The B
Ministry

Godly Principles to Protect Your Ministry
From Pitfalls and Burnout

By Dr. Daniel Daves

Mighty Eagle Publishing
Mansfield, TX

Ministry Recommendations

"A person could save many hours just by reading this book. It's like the Reader's Digest Condensed Books - cuts to the chase without getting side-tracked along the way. This would be a very helpful tool for anyone in ministry indeed."

— Dr. James Maloney

"The vibrant organizational ideas of Dr. Daniel Daves' *The Business of Ministry* fill an integral need in our churches that has long needed addressing. Brimming with ground breaking, innovative ideas, it is one smart book you and your church won't want to do without. I highly recommend his book to all churches who seek to better serve their congregations and their communities in Christ's name. "

— Don Stewart

"A book that couples much needed wisdom in the matters of stewardship and spiritual understanding, in both local church and kingdom application. Valuable reading for pastors, church leaders and Christian business entrepreneurs. I highly recommend this book. "

— Dr. Don Matison

Recommendation From Author
Tom Leding

"The Spirit of the Lord is upon me: because the Lord hath anointed me to preach"... Isaiah 61:1-3

I am so happy that you are holding this book in your hands today. It reveals your desire to improve your ministry, become knowledgeable, and become your best in the Kingdom of God.

How would you like to spend a few evenings with one of the greatest ministers of our day just picking his brain? Well, I've spent time with my good friend, Dr. Daniel Daves, doing just that, asking the same questions he has covered in his great book, *"The Business of Ministry."*

"O" how I wish I had had a book like this when I went into the ministry. It would have saved me some sleepless nights.

Ahead of you stretches your future, like a road leading into the distance. Along that road are ambitions you wish to accomplish... desires you wish to gratify. To bring your ambitions and desires to fulfillment, you must be successful with your ministry.

Use the principles made clear in the pages which follow, let them guide you away from the problems you will encounter as a minister of the Gospel. *"The Business of Ministry"* will help you to have the fuller, happier life God intended you to have.

By the time you have moved through all the pages you may decide to go through them again. Wonderful! The plan is simple, but it's all up to you and God.

Tom Leding
Author of the best selling books...
   "Rags To Riches... You Don't Have To Be Poor No More"
   "The Making Of A King" and
   "Prosperity Is Your Inheritance"

"The Business of Ministry"

Godly Principles to Protect Your Ministry From Pitfalls and Burnout

Quotes From This Book –

MAKING MINISTRY FUN -
Ministry is the highest calling on the planet and is also one of the hardest. It's taxing on a human being to be caring for other's need, sin, trouble and tragedy. If you don't MAKE your ministry fun and exciting, you will quite possibly go crazy or get embittered and lose your ministry destiny.

CREATIVE 21ST CENTURY FUND RAISING -
Car wash money is hard money to earn. At the end of a hard working hot day in the sun, the 20 of you made $200 before you take out the cost of soap, food and drinks. You all could have worked for $1.00 an hour somewhere and made as much money for your youth ministry without inheriting the sunburn. We don't do youth car washes anymore. We have seed money!

PROTECTING YOUR TREASURER -
If there's a bill that's late, don't make your church treasurer explain "why" it's late. This is your ministry. You must get involved and explain to those that you're delinquent with. This protection is a must for the spiritual and mental health of your treasurer. Remember, they're keeping and watching the treasury for you, but they are not the one in final authority over the treasury. You are that authority.

Dr. Daniel Daves is an international conference speaker to business and spiritual leaders as well as to Christians abroad. He is the president of Children's Feeding Network, helping to rescue needy children from tragedy worldwide.

Dr. Daniel Daves

Conference Speaker

Dr. Daves is available on a limited schedule for speaking engagements, college classes and leadership training seminars.

You may contact Dr. Daves at
info@childrensfeedingnetwork.org

Published By:
Mighty Eagle Publishing
#8 Calloway Ct.
Mansfield, TX 76063

Email:
info@mightyeagle.com

Web Sites:
www.mightyeagle.com

www.basicsforsuccess.com

Table Of Contents

The Business Of Ministry
Copyright © 2004 by Mighty Eagle Publishing
ISBN # 0-9763521-0-9
Published by Mighty Eagle Publishing, Dallas, TX, U.S.A.
www.mightyeagle.com
Cover design by Wendy Selvig
Picture of pastor carrying church by Brian Tressler, CFN Missionary

Unless otherwise indicated, all scripture quotations are taken from the King James Version of the Bible.

NOTICE: This publication is designed to provide accurate and authoritative information in regard to the subject matter covered. It is sold with the understanding that the publisher is not engaged in rendering legal, accounting, or other professional services. If legal advice or other expert assistance is required, the services of a competent professional person should be sought.

. . . From the Declaration of Principles jointly adopted by a Committee of the American Bar Association and a Committee of Publishers and Associations.

Dedication

This book is dedicated first to Jesus Christ who has given me the ability to share the wisdom in this book. He has held me by the hand while I walked out and learned these principles (many in the valley of the shadow of death), and He gave me spiritual fathers and many mentors who have imparted their best and deepest into my life. For that, I dedicate this book to my Lord Jesus.

Secondly, I dedicate this book to my dear wife Tracy who has walked along side of me through years of ministry. Her love, acceptance, encouragement, laughter, joy and wisdom has helped me to learn the valuable lessons in this book at an accelerated pace that only a virtuous woman can bring. Thank you, my love!

Thirdly, I dedicate this book to the innocent, stricken, crushed and abandoned children around the world who have no voice, no parent and no one to cry out to for help. May this book empower the great men and women of God to find you and bring God's mercy, compassion and help to you in Jesus' name!

Deep Appreciation

My deepest thanks go to my spiritual fathers, Dr. Don Matison and Don Stewart. Your deep impartations have made me all that I am today. Thanks to my family, wife and children who have sacrificed and given so that I could fulfill the call of God on my life over these last years. Thank you, Wendy for your awesome proof reading and cutting edge critiquing of this book. Thanks also for the beautiful cover work that you designed under inspiration of the Holy Spirit. God bless you!

The Business of Ministry

Preface

Before getting started with the *"Business of Ministry"*, I am assuming that you have already experienced or strongly sensed the "calling" of God upon your life to be a minister in His service. This "calling" is a most precious and holy blessing, as the sovereign Creator of Heaven and earth has called you into service for His eternal purposes.

I found early in my ministry that God doesn't operate His ministry like an earthly corporation, businesses or some man's idea of democratic board run hierarchy. He is holy and the government of His ministry is holy and eternal. His servants must also be holy (set apart from the world). His operations and ministry movements cannot be confined to a typical corporate setting. A true servant of God can't simply operate a ministry like an earthly business or corporation. There are certain biblical principles and methods of operation that we must learn if we are to be successful in ministry. The "Business of the Ministry" is designed to help you understand how God releases creativity and heavenly design in strategic key areas where you will be making decisions. It will also save you from multiple burn out possibilities because your ministry will be developed decently and in order with protective measures to help you prosper under the proper covering of kingdom ministry business principles.

Lastly, this book will help you to find solid answers to general ministry business situations, structures, legal, financial and tax help issues that commonly arise in a ministry after you've been through bible college, seminary or formal training.

If you've heard the saying, "That's none of your business", that statement is true of anyone not called into the holy and set apart ministry of God. Ministry is serious business! It's literally

God's business on earth. May we humbly seek His ways and thoughts in every ministry business matter. We can trust that the God will teach us, as the anointing will teach us all things.

1 John 2:27 But the anointing which ye have received of him abideth in you, and ye need not that any man teach you: but as the same anointing teacheth you of all things, and is truth, and is no lie, and even as it hath taught you, ye shall abide in him.

This book is written for all who find themselves serving God in His ministry or desiring to do so. It addresses many normal and every day areas where a business decision must be made correctly for God and His Kingdom purpose. I attempt to shed light on ministry business situations and have added some actual life scenarios so that you might be better informed when put in the position of having to make critical ministry decisions. I have accumulated this wisdom and information from 20+ years of pastoral experience and many wonderful spiritual fathers and mentors who gave me wisdom in critical times. I pray that this information helps to guide you in your times of ministry challenges that are definitely going to come.

Chapter One
Honor

In this chapter, we will discuss honor in many different aspects of ministry. We'll discuss how to have honor in your relationship with God and His ministry, your spiritual father, your authorities, your staff members, and money.

The ministry of Jesus Christ is one of great honor. Anyone who walks into this holy calling must walk in the principle of honor. Honor spreads from your relationship with God to earthly relationships with your spouse, children, church, governing officials and authorities, and people in your community. Ministers fail miserably without the spirit of honor in their character.

FIRST THINGS – PUTTING GOD FIRST

There is a set order to everything in life. It's God's desire that we place Him first in everything. For the servant of Jesus Christ, putting God first in your personal life and ministry is imperative for success. There is no true success possible without putting God first in your life. Now is the time to start!

- God said to bring the best of your *"first"* fruits as an offering to Him.

- Jesus said to seek ye *"first"* the Kingdom of God and His righteousness.

- Jesus said that if you're bringing an offering to God, to go *"first"* and be restored to your brother whom you have ought.

What you do *"first"* is a key to who you are. What is your *"first"* reaction to a problem or circumstance? What is the *"first"* thing that you do when you get up in the morning? Who do you go to *"first"* when you have a situation that needs attention?

You honor God by putting Him first, and by going to Him first. We need to honor Him daily by seeking Him first every day.

As you seek to better your ministry, I recommend that you first join the 5 O'clock club with me. This club will keep your spiritual character in check every day and will help you to focus on your vision while continually developing your solid character trait.

My dear friend and a wonderful financial minister, Rev. Tom Leding has a web site where you can join the 5 O'clock club free of charge. Go to www.tomleding.com and join it now. Once you're a member, you'll be committing with the rest of us to do the following FIRST when you get up in the morning:

1. Pray and ask God to illuminate His Word to you.
2. Read 2 old testament chapters of the bible
3. Read 5 Psalms chapters
4. Read 2 Proverbs chapters
5. Read 2 new testament chapters of the bible
6. Pray and read over your written goals

The 5 O'clock club has dramatically changed every life of the people I know including my own. I've seen it bless my own household dramatically. It seems too simple, but it really works. Your life will never be the same. Join the club and put the Word of God first in your life from now on. What a great character trait you will possess in just a few weeks of obedience! The light that will come into your heart and soul will dramatically bring you into prosperity, increase and divine destiny towards ministry and servant hood!

GOD AND HIS MINISTRY

1 Tim 5:19 - 20 Against an elder receive not an accusation, but before two or three witnesses. Them that sin rebuke before all, that others also may fear.

While pastoring for many years, it's interesting how many times I'd hear terrible things about the other men of God in my community. Mostly it was just innuendo from people who were taking an illicit jab at a pastor because they didn't agree with him, they'd gotten hurt by someone in his church, or just because they are critical people. I would simply try to calm these people and pat them on the back saying, "It's going to be OK". But then I started realizing that there was a verbal assault going on against God's men. These men of God were being slaughtered with words by critical, foolish people who were ignorantly bringing God's judgment upon themselves. I was listening to this judgment and because I didn't confront it openly, I was receiving it and agreeing with it in principle. This was beginning to bring God's judgment upon me as well. Six months into my first senior pastor position, I had started considering how bad and terrible these other men of God must be in my new home city because these accusers were so hurt and offended. I had began a withdrawal in my heart from these men of God (whom I didn't even know personally), and the devil began to get a foothold in my life.

3

The Business Of Ministry

Heb 12:15 Looking diligently lest any man fail of the grace of God; lest any root of bitterness springing up trouble you, and thereby many be defiled;

By not confronting these slanderers and accusers, I was in agreement with their bitterness and it would soon defile me and my entire ministry, church and family if I didn't get cleansed from this. This is where God taught me the required principle of "Honor 101".

Through my daily prayer I began to see my weakness and sin in this matter. I found myself accusatory of other long standing churches and ministries that I didn't even know anything about. I repented and asked God to help me understand this deceptive tactic of the enemy and my own old natural self *(our prideful old man nature loves controversy, strife and slander)*. God taught me to honor my fellow servants of God whether I knew them or not, and whether I agreed fully with them or not. I began to pray for these men of God in my community, and years later though I still don't know some of them, I feel like a very good friend of theirs because I love them dearly. I support and honor them for their lives given into the ministry calling of Christ. I honor a man or woman of God for his/her commitment, warfare and tenacity. I honor a pastor for putting himself on the front line with Christ and constantly caring for a group of sheep no matter what the size of the flock. I love these people and I now know how to honor them! I also don't put up with slander or abusive innuendo from slanderers and accusers.

Honor is a vital part of any Christian ministry and honor must be a character trait of the headship or leadership of any ministry. Without honor in your heart, you can never train and disciple people into honor. You and I will either reproduce people of honor or dishonor, depending on what's in our own hearts. Therefore, develop the character trait of honor in your own life and ministry as well as in your ministry leadership team. If you have a problem with slander, defamation of character or an accusatory spirit, get yourself free from it now! Having this

4

dishonoring spirit will destroy your life, marriage, family, ministry and future destiny.

Never speak evil of another.   Simply put, if you can't speak good about a person, don't speak at all.

I know a great man of God who is clearly God's friend and he hates slander with a passion.   He will openly rebuke you and walk out in the middle of your dinner, business meeting or any fellowship if you begin to talk evil or slanderous of any leader in his presence.   He is simply not interested in hearing your critical opinion of another, and he will let you know it, rebuking publicly as I Tim. 5:20 commands.   Because of this, God has honored this man and his ministry.   It seems that everyone knows of this man's character trait.   People don't bring slanderous, filthy accusation about others to him anymore because they fear being rebuked and walked out on. Praise God! Would to God that we all could be like this!

Mat 12:37   For by thy words thou shalt be justified, and by thy words thou shalt be condemned.

Be careful what you say in the presence of God!   It's by your words that you are justified or condemned.   When you judge, you are judging yourself *(Matt. 7:1 - 2)*.   If you speak evil about any man or woman of God, or anyone in authority, you license others around you to speak evil of you and you authorize a destructive spirit that's not from God.   Those under your authority are given the right to destroy you when they choose, because you have shown them how to destroy others when you choose.   God commands us not to destroy!

Honor requires that we honor God, His gifts, His servants and those in authority.   Honor them whether or not you believe in their theology, ideas or their understanding of the Word of God. They're His servants, not yours.   It's His place to judge and correct, and He is well able to speak to His servants and direct

5

them into His perfect will. He is also well able to take care of those who are false.

Develop a ministry policy concerning honor and unfounded accusatory slander or defamation. Implement the "Three Strikes And You're Out" policy, warning any and all staff members that accusation is grounds for dismissal. Anyone caught in habitual slander and accusation is a person of dishonor and will bring constant reproach and judgment on your ministry. Protect the ministry, your staff members, your volunteers, your vision and your future. Don't jeopardize the great calling of God on your life for any resentful or bitter employee who can't seem to find honor as an utmost important part of life.

Heb 12:15 KJV Looking diligently lest any man fail of the grace of God; lest any root of bitterness springing up trouble you, and thereby many be defiled;

FINDING YOUR SPIRITUAL FATHER

Eph 6:2 - 3 Honour thy father and mother; which is the first commandment with promise; That it may be well with thee, and thou mayest live long on the earth.

Honor is the bedrock of ministry. In a darkened world of dishonor, someone must show the character trait of honor. Honoring your father and mother is imperative. This includes both natural and spiritual parents.

If you're in ministry today, then you really must have a spiritual father, or at least be in pursuit of one.

1 Cor 4:15 For though ye have ten thousand instructors in Christ, yet have ye not many fathers: for in Christ Jesus I have begotten you through the gospel.

Paul said that you have not many fathers. Mal. 4:5 - 6 calls for a great return of fathers and sons, or a curse resides in the land because of the lack of honor displayed in the spiritual family relationship. Any valid ministry in this day must set themselves on a mission to find their spiritual father. Why?

Anointing from God flows down from Fathers to sons. In the Old Testament, God told Moses to anoint Aaron and his sons for ministry *(Ex. 30:30)*. Moses anointed Aaron as the high priest by anointing his head with oil. This oil flowed from his head down onto his beard and onto his robes. There was plenty of oil used in this anointing service!

When it was time for Aaron the high priest to pass the ministry on to his son, he took off the anointed robe and put it onto his son who had trained faithfully under him. There was a passing of anointing from father to son.

Elijah threw his mantle upon Elisha and began a father – son relationship that would soon deliver a double portion onto Elisha as he cried "My Father, My Father" while Elijah was being taken up.

Time and space refrains me from showing the New Testament fulfillment of this Old Testament principle. However, it is still vitally important that we in ministry walk in the spirit of honor and find our spiritual father. God is into family, fathers and sons. There is a covering, an anointing and a heritage that is passed down through spiritual father – son relationships.

Anyone who is not in pursuit of finding his spiritual ministry father will find that he has entered a bastard ministry *(bastard = one who has no father),* and one that is unable to receive or walk in the anointing of true Holy Spirit ministry in the last day revival and harvest activities of God.

I believe that God has winced at our ignorance in the past, and He has used many great men who have never had a spiritual father. However, I believe that father/son ministry relationships will be vital in fulfilling our commission on this earth in the near future. I don't want anyone to think that they can't be used of the Holy Spirit, or that I'm nullifying anyone's ministry who doesn't have a spiritual father, passing them off as a non Spirit led ministry. However, the scriptures are clear that the anointing of the priesthood flows downward from fathers to sons.

Our Heavenly Father anointed His Son Jesus. Jesus anointed His ministry sons (the apostles). They anointed their ministry sons, their disciples. I understand that there is a heavenly anointing to all who are in Christ Jesus, as we are all sons of God through Him and in Him who loved us and gave Himself for us. However, there is also a natural father-son return that God is calling for on this earth, indicated in Malachi 4. These fathers spoken of are spiritual fathers that Paul spoke of in I Cor. 4:15.

We must honor our spiritual father once he is found. He is worthy of our love, prayers, time and finances. He might be the one that you and your ministry tithes "UPWARD" to. *(See Tithing Chapter)*. He is to be honored and cared for in his older age, and he is to be acknowledged by his sons and daughters regardless of how good or bad things are going with his ministry. If you've accelerated past his effectiveness in ministry, praise God! This is the plan of any good spiritual father. Any Elijah wants his Elisha to double his anointing and ministry abilities. However, just because you are more successful than your spiritual father does not give you any right to forsake or dishonor him in any way.

Eph 6:2 - 3 Honour thy father and mother; which is the first commandment with promise; That it may be well with thee, and thou mayest live long on the earth.

Find your spiritual father. Honor his birthdays, anniversary, his wife's birthday, his accomplishments, and you personally be the one to give him a 30th, 40th, 50th ministry anniversary honoring party. Do it up big with honor. Spend the money that's

8

necessary to make it a true honoring event. Remember, as you do it unto your spiritual father, you are doing it unto God Himself! He's watching you, and to the measure that you honor your father, that is the measure that you will be honored by God and your staff, wife, children and congregation.

If you don't have a spiritual father, and know very little about this, I recommend that you go to our web site to get further reference materials on spiritual fathers. Also read the book *"You Have Not Many Fathers"* by Dr. Mark Hanby. You can get our materials and this book at www.basicsforsuccess.com. Dr. Hanby's book is a "MUST" for any minister's book shelf and should be read once per year in my opinion.

SUBMISSION TO AUTHORITY

God wants us to first be sons, then to be fathers. There are no fathers who were not first sons. It is a hard thing for you to become a spiritual father unless you are first a spiritual son.

The first principle in becoming a spiritual son is submission to authority. When you submit to the authorities that God has placed in and around your life, then you can be trusted with a spiritual father who you will honor and respect.

Heb 13:17 Obey them that have the rule over you, and submit yourselves: for they watch for your souls, as they that must give account, that they may do it with joy, and not with grief: for that is unprofitable for you.

Responding correctly to authority opens up many doors for a person who understands and honors this powerful principle. God has placed authority in the earth for us to work under, not around. In other words, He is not looking to bless people who find ways to get around authority. He blesses those who work under His authority.

The Business Of Ministry

1 Pet 2:13 - 17 Submit yourselves to every ordinance of man for the Lord's sake: whether it be to the king, as supreme; Or unto governors, as unto them that are sent by him for the punishment of evildoers, and for the praise of them that do well. For so is the will of God, that with well doing ye may put to silence the ignorance of foolish men: As free, and not using your liberty for a cloak of maliciousness, but as the servants of God. Honour all men. Love the brotherhood. Fear God. Honour the king.

Authority is cleverly disguised in many packages. However, behind the package is God Himself who tests you to see if you will obey in the little things. The little things are authorities who are set over your life, whether the government of man or of the church.

Mat 25:21 His lord said unto him, Well done, thou good and faithful servant: thou hast been faithful over a few things, I will make thee ruler over many things: enter thou into the joy of thy lord.

There are two secret doors that will open to a person who's submitted to authority. These doors keep the wicked out of the realm that they don't belong. However, if a person can pass through these two doors of testing, manifest Heavenly authority is granted to give this believer the same authority on earth that Jesus Himself walked in. This includes healing the sick, raising the dead, cleansing the leper, making the blind see and the lame walk. It also includes a host of miraculous operations of wisdom, financial blessing and knowledge that are hidden from those who cannot submit to authority. The two doors are called:

1. Man's authority, and
2. Spiritual/church authority.

How do you respond to your government and the laws of the land which are over you and your ministry? *(I'm not talking about lawless law where governments make laws that stand opposed to the law giver and the 10 commandments. Of course,*

The Business Of Ministry

we are not to submit to any law that would violate our faith and religious frieedoms.) Do you pay your taxes, drive the speed limit, honor the badge of a police officer and refuse to speak evil of an elected official, law maker, judge, king or president? Do you produce a manifested, active submission to man's authority in your life? Do you submit to a pastor or have leaders in your life and ministry that have authority over you? These are the "little things" that will cause God to take note and bless you with true authority yourself.

Authority Tip:
No servant of God will ever possess true authority without first and always being submitted to authority. The moment you lose your submission, you also lose your authority.

Once a person walks in submission to natural authorities, God will then give an opportunity towards submission to spiritual authority. The willingness and ability to submit to God's spiritual authorities will determine a person's true dominion in this life. Submission and authority is serious business with God. Our very lives and destinies depend on success in this area. God's kingdom-blessings don't flow towards those who cannot submit.

If you find yourself walking in the continued spirit of non-submission, then you will find yourself written about in the bible, labeled by God Himself as ungodly, a rebel, a usurper, one who opposes and who denies our Lord Jesus Christ. You may say to Him, "Lord, Lord, did I not do these great things?" and He will say to you, *"Away from me, I never knew you"*.

Ungodly rebels, usurpers, opposers and deniers of Christ are closely related in their actions with Satan himself. The lack of submission to authority gives Satan's dark kingdom it's strength.

11

Jude 1:3, 4 . . .and exhort you that ye should earnestly contend for the faith which was once delivered unto the saints. For there are certain men crept in unawares, who were before of old ordained to this condemnation, ungodly men, turning the grace of our God into lasciviousness, and denying the only Lord God, and our Lord Jesus Christ.

*Jude 1:8 Likewise also these filthy dreamers defile the flesh, **despise dominion**, and speak evil of dignities.*

Jude 1:11 - 13 Woe unto them! for they have gone in the way of Cain, and ran greedily after the error of Balaam for reward, and perished in the gainsaying of Core. These are spots in your feasts of charity, when they feast with you, feeding themselves without fear: clouds they are without water, carried about of winds; trees whose fruit withereth, without fruit, twice dead, plucked up by the roots; Raging waves of the sea, foaming out their own shame; wandering stars, to whom is reserved the blackness of darkness for ever.

The scriptures warn believers about non submitted people in their churches and communities. God makes it clear that these people are not flowing in the Spirit of Christ and are not a true part of Christ's dominion.

Some people attempt to justify their rebellious behavior because they don't like the one in charge, or they have a personality conflict with the person whom God has given authority to. Some walk in accusation against governments, churches and authorities and that accusative spirit keeps them from submitting. However, God is not interested in whether or not you like the person, the official, the pastor or the judge. Personality is not the issue. He wants to know if you honor the authority that has been set upon that person.

> **Food For Thought:**
> *If you base your submission to authority upon whether or not you like the personality of your pastor, your boss or a police officer, what happens when you stand before Jesus Christ and find that you have a personality conflict with Him?*

Anyone can submit when things are going your way and when the authority is in agreement with you. But the true test of submission comes when the authority disagrees with you, your plans, your thoughts or actions. Can you submit, change your course and repent in order to line up with your authority? That is a test that each of us will go through. I pray that we all pass this test.

Our God is one of dominion (authority). He is a great King. His Kingdom is a domain. His promises are part of his dominion. His people belong to Him. His governing order is set to bring His dominion into the earth from Heaven. He needs men and women who will submit to authority whether they like the one in authority or not. If you can submit to God's authorities, you are ready to possess true authority. You are also in position to honor a spiritual father, and God knows that He can place a spiritual father in your life.

I recommend Watchman Nee's book called *"Spiritual Authority"* which is a must for any minister's book shelf. You can find this book at www.basicsforsuccess.com. This book changed my life and positioned me for the great blessings that have come into my life and ministry as I came into an understanding of submission to authority.

There is further information also available on this subject in chapter 5 of this book under the heading *"Extreme Personal Accountability"*.

HONORING THOSE WHO LABOR WITH YOU

One of the things that all people need sowed into their lives is honor. They must know that what they are doing is appreciated, honored and accepted. Even the toughest old guy that doesn't need a pat on the back MUST know that his work is valued and appreciated. I know many people who will not give their time, talents, gifts and finances into certain ministries and churches simply because they know it wouldn't be honored or utilized correctly. Therefore that ministry suffers needlessly because if they would simply learn the meaning of the word *"Honor"*, they would have all of the volunteers and finances that they need.

Honoring those who labor among you is very important. Make a list now of all of your staff members and volunteers. Consider what they do for you and the ministry. Whether paid or not, are these people satisfied and honored, knowing that their input and hard work is deeply appreciated? Remember, it's easy for a person to know that God appreciates their work (*if they have a very close personal relationship with Him*). However, if they are looking to you for leadership, and if they're following you as you follow Christ, then they are looking to you for honor as well.

"Recognition of worth is like 1,000 paychecks to a volunteer!" There's nothing that can replace the feeling of worth, value and a sense that you have accomplished something for God. It's our job to make sure that our staff and volunteers feel this way continually.

As our ministry grows, we have new programs, volunteers and staff continually giving into our ministry in various ways. The last time I counted, we had around 30 programs in operation in our ministry. Each program has a leader and a group of volunteers. In order to not become weary and overwhelmed, we wrote down each ministry and then decided that we would start honoring the staff and volunteers over each ministry at least once per year. We decided to use our Sunday AM service as the platform to honor these different ministries in front of everyone.

Therefore about half of our services throughout the year would have a 10 minute time of honor and explanation of the specific ministry and the staff. As we began to look at each ministry, we hand picked specific times that each ministry would be honored. Our *"Summer Teen Discipleship"* program ends in August, and therefore we honor all of the Summer workers at the end of August. Our *"Youth Music Video TV Show"* finalizes a year's worth of programming in September, so we honor them at the end of September. The Praise and Worship team works very hard during the holidays to bring the best music ministry possible, so we honor their hard work in January right after the new year. Many ministries are ongoing and continual so we fit them into the schedule to keep an even flow of honor throughout the year.

This is the least that we can do to publicly honor our staff and volunteers. They're working hard for the glory of God and we the church must be appreciative and honoring of their work. We must value their giving or it will be taken away from us. What we don't value we will lose.

Keep the spirit of honor at the forefront of your staff and volunteers. It will cause them to grow with a sense of honor too, and they will continue to honor what is important and valuable in their lives. They will recognize that you honor them and in this dark day of dishonor in the land, they will draw closer and closer to your ministry.

Throw an occasional surprise party for your volunteers of a certain program once in awhile. Stand up and tell them why you are doing it. Tell them of your deep appreciation for their sacrifice, their hard work and their commitment to Christ. It will be the best pizza ever purchased, and will gain new and closer followers to your ministry.

Also, make sure that you send birthday and anniversary cards to your staff and volunteers. There are many programs and online services who will remind you of birthdays and when it's time to write and send a card.

Honoring your workers is a fun and rewarding opportunity to sow value and worth into their lives.

HONOR AND RESPECT FOR EVERY DOLLAR THAT COMES TO YOU

We've learned to respect the funds that come into our hands, as every dollar represents someone's life.

I have a prosperous ministry friend who taught me how to handle money. He showed me how he had his people work with the dollar bills. I was watching this man's staff count an offering after a revival one night. They were unfolding each bill, straightening any bent or folded corners of the bills, and putting them all in order, face up and in nice piles. These old bills looked like they had been given a face lift and the piles were equally stacked in orderly amounts. They were nicely rubber banded together and looked like they were worthy to be coming straight out of the bank vault.

Then this man told me a secret. He said, "I treat my money with respect and care. I have found that if I treat this money with the highest respect, then this money will call it's other money friends to come my way. Money deserves respect and it won't come to those who don't respect it."

We kind of chuckled at the comment but I knew that he was onto something. I started implementing this spirit of respect into our ministry and the offerings and fund raisers jumped in value immediately. Other finances started finding their way into our hands as well because of our new found respect for them. I believe that this secret is a powerful, yet simple truth that causes

16

more money to come supernaturally. I don't know how it works, I just know that it works.

If you have ever read the book "The Richest Man In Babylon", you would learn from this book that this principle is true. All money is here to serve us. However, money wants to serve the best masters. If you can't keep a $1 Washington bill nicely folded and cared for, why should Mr. Jackson, Mr. Franklin or Mr. Jefferson come your way?

Chapter 1 Review Points

- Put God first in every day.
- Pray for other ministers and spiritual leaders.
- Determine to find your spiritual father.
- Submit to all authorities.
- Appreciate those who labor among you.
- Respect money.

Chapter Two
Vision

VISION CASTING
DEVELOPING AND WORKING THE LONG TERM
PLAN

It is so vitally important to have personal long term goals as well as church/ministry long term goals. We must work our vision and purpose every day. Repetition and focus are the keys to success in God's ministry. However, if we don't VISION CAST or keep our eye on the horizon with long term goals in mind, we can lose track of the true purpose of the ministry. I know many people who have lost 5 – 10 years of their lives because they forgot to look forward into their future. They were so busy building the daily road and they never looked up to see if they were building it straight. They built themselves right into a dead end ally with no place to go.

You might be performing daily ministry assignments, and your schedule might be set for the next year with Microsoft Outlook ringing bells and whistles every day. You might have your routine set each day for the rest of your life, and that's important. However if you don't have the larger picture in mind while you do these things, you will most certainly build off course and off of your destiny.

Vision casting is vitally important to hitting your target goal. Where do you plan to be in 20 years? What goals, desires and dreams do you plan to have accomplished by then? What are some of the amazing things that you want to accomplish which will take the next 20 years of planning? Keep these things in front of you and remind yourself of them at least weekly.

The Business Of Ministry

Your daily and weekly grind of ministry MUST be building towards your 20 year goals and plans. If not, then you are building your ministry into a dead end alley. There will be a day that you wake up and realize that your life is coming to an end and you are nowhere near your final purpose in life and ministry.

Vision Casting – keeping the dream ever before your weekly, monthly and yearly view.

You don't know what your 20 year plans, desires and dreams are? It's time to fast and pray, write down your goals and dreams and get the plan from God who gives freely to all who ask.

GOAL SETTING – MINISTRY EVALUATION

It's very important that you as a leader learn to set and define goals for your personal life and ministry. I've heard that 90% of the world doesn't set goals while 10% of the world does set goals. The result is that 10% of the world owns 90% of the world's wealth and riches. Don't be another failed ministry that fits into the 90% category. Your people need a leader who can teach and disciple them to become goal setters. No one deserves to be led down the road of poverty and lack. You're the one who must rise to the occasion, set and maintain your goals, and teach your staff and people to also set and maintain goals for their lives.

Psa 37:4-5 Delight thyself also in the LORD; and he shall give thee the desires of thine heart. Commit thy way unto the LORD; trust also in him; and he shall bring it to pass.

Goals are closely related to vision. They're a future vision cast of what is to come. None of us know exactly what is coming in the future, but we do know that God puts desires in our hearts so that we will chase after them. Therefore, your desires and dreams are closely related to God's divine will in your life.

20

Therefore you must learn to focus, discipline and restrain them under His direction and leading.

Take time and begin to dream. Write down your goals, desires and dreams for the next 1,5, 10 and 20 years. Remember that many Japanese business people plan for 150 years from now. Many of them are working their great grandfather's vision right now. You're only starting with a 20 year plan that's still within your generation.

Don't be afraid to dream and vision cast. Your fulfillment in life will include reaching your goals and dreams. If you don't have any active goals set, you're surely not going to hit them. I can guarantee that the captain of a large ship will never hit the port of his dreams if he doesn't make some plans to sail that way. You're sure to never hit the goals that you never set.

Apply this next section first for your personal life, and then for your ministry.

My top 3 goals for this next year:

1._____

2._____

3._____

My top 3 goals for the next 5 years:

1._____

2._____

3._____

My top 3 goals for the next 10 years:

1._____

2._____

3._____

My top 3 goals for the next 20 years:

1._____

2._____

3._____

Once you pray over your goals and set them into place, you now have something to shoot for as an individual, a minister and with your ministry team. Meet frequently with your staff to see what needs to be done next to reach these goals. Take pro-active steps to accomplish these goals. Ask God to open doors for you. Make decisions in light of your goals. Don't get side tracked and off course. Look at your one and five year goals daily. Look at your 10 year goals weekly, and your 20 year goals monthly. Always set each day to do something towards your goals. Build with consistency, discipline and fervency.

As you get further revelation from God you might need to modify a goal. Go ahead and do it. However, keep the goals in front of you and get your entire church and team working daily to fulfill these goals. Imagine the multiplication of having your entire church or ministry staff working daily to accomplish your vision and goals. You'll be amazed at the corporate power of one! If one hundred can put ten thousand to flight, then imagine what you all can do together!!!

Lev 26:8   And five of you shall chase an hundred, and an hundred of you shall put ten thousand to flight: and your enemies shall fall before you by the sword.

I believe that goal setting is a very important part of character building, discipline and leadership. None of your people (including yourself) deserve to be in the 90% category of people who don't set goals and who end up with minimal fulfilled destiny. You must get your team into the top 10% category. Start today and never stop!

Once you get used to working a 20 year plan, you need to consider a realistic 150 year plan which will span the lives of your children, grandchildren and great grandchildren. This will give you true multi-generational purpose and will absolutely change the way you make decisions, spend your time and focus your energies on earth.

Take a moment right now and write a paragraph or two that states your dream for your future generations and what you'd like to see them doing with the anointing, wisdom, vision and knowledge that you've imparted into them.

_____

_____

_____

_____

_____

_____

_____

_____

_____

_____

_____

_____

_____

_____

_____

_____

_____

_____

_____

_____

_____

_____

_____

_____

_____

_____

_____

_____

_____

_____

_____

_____

_____

_____

_____

DEVELOPING A PROFESSIONAL BUSINESS PLAN

Prov 29:18 Where there is no vision, the people perish . . .

Once you are well on your way to writing down your vision and developing your ministry goals and plans, it's time to put together a professional business plan that people and professionals can read and envision. This business plan will help you state the vision clearly. It will also give the general guidelines of who you are and what you do. It will help you keep focused and on track. It will also empower others to find themselves within your business plan so they can help you build the vision.

It's good for every ministry to develop and maintain a business plan just like a business would. This is the document that you can go back to in order to evaluate your ministry. With this document in place you can see if you're succeeding in your stated goals and vision. You will see if you need to make changes in order to bring success and fruit.

By the way, God wrote down His business plan. We call it the Holy bible.

You can go to our web site and download a free business plan template that will help you to format your business plan correctly. Go to www.basicsforsuccess.com.

Chapter 2 Review Points

- Develop a long term vision.
- Commit to set and maintain daily goals.
- Develop a professional ministry business plan.

Chapter Three
Governing organizational Law

GOD'S NEW TESTAMENT GOVERNING STRUCTURE

The following chapter contains revelational New Testament information that will progress any ministry from it's current status to the cutting edge of Heaven's plan of ministry government on earth. The author understands that each ministry is in a current governmental pattern of one type or another, and there is no condemnation or critical judgment of any of these patterns. It is also recognized that if it were not for these governmental patterns bringing us to this 21st century in Christ's ministry, we'd never be able to enter into the "more excellent" way of ministry. In your place of transition and paradigm shifting towards greater excellence in Christ, please understand that Christ Himself will lead you to the open doors of God's governmental change. Just as the high priest had to completely change clothing to enter the most holy place once per year under God's direction, so Christ will direct us how to change in actuality, our governmental coverings so that we may be qualified to enter the glorious earthly reality of His third dimensional, third room, holy of holies type experience.

Mat 6:10 Thy kingdom come. Thy will be done in earth, as it is in heaven.

To be successful in God's ministry, we must understand His divine order and New Testament requirements for ministry on earth. God's government is not like man's. It's much higher and

27

carries the eternal power of Heaven with it. If we set God's governmental order in place on earth just as Moses set the tabernacle in the wilderness, He will fill the ministry with Heavenly power and authority.

If an electrician wires a house wrong, he will burn the house down when the power switch is thrown. This is why there is very little earthly power and Heavenly authority in the church today. The house is wired wrong. If God were to throw the power switch and fill the house with His presence, power and glorious authority, the house would burn to the ground and the ministry would be destroyed.

Luke 5:37 - 39 And no man putteth new wine into old bottles; else the new wine will burst the bottles, and be spilled, and the bottles shall perish. But new wine must be put into new bottles; and both are preserved. No man also having drunk old wine straightway desireth new: for he saith, The old is better.

We must wire the house correctly if we want God's power in our New Testament ministry. God's governmental order is worthy of the study of multiple books on the subject. However in this book I will give you simple basics, historical facts and *"wiring instructions"* for Heaven's New Testament ministry on earth.

Every kingdom or nation has a government. That government has rules, statutes and laws that govern that kingdom or nation. The Kingdom of God is no different, and it has it's own set of spiritual laws, statutes, rules and methods of operation. We would do well to learn these quickly before getting too far in ministry, as we are to be ambassadors of this great kingdom.

The apostle Paul stated clearly how the governing authority of the church was to be set by God:

Eph 4:11 - 16 And he gave some, apostles; and some, prophets; and some, evangelists; and some, pastors and teachers; For the perfecting of the saints, for the work of the ministry, for the

28

edifying of the body of Christ: Till we all come in the unity of the faith, and of the knowledge of the Son of God, unto a perfect man, unto the measure of the stature of the fullness of Christ: That we henceforth be no more children, tossed to and fro, and carried about with every wind of doctrine, by the sleight of men, and cunning craftiness, whereby they lie in wait to deceive; But speaking the truth in love, may grow up into him in all things, which is the head, even Christ: From whom the whole body fitly joined together and compacted by that which every joint supplieth, according to the effectual working in the measure of every part, maketh increase of the body unto the edifying of itself in love.

The five fold New Testament ministry consists of five governmental pillars of support. There is an biblical type and shadow of this governmental gift looking at the Old Testament tabernacle of Moses. Five pillars stand at the entrance of the holy place, and every priest must enter by going through these pillars. Five also numerically consists of the grace of God in the bible.

We see that if the governing authority is set correctly in the ministry, then there are many blessings that will come of it. Included is perfection and maturity of the saints, the work of the ministry by the saints, edification of the body in love, unity among the brethren, intimate relationship with Jesus, and the blessing of a lighter load among the ministry.

I can tell you from experience that there's nothing worse than trying to keep a weak willed, fleshly minded, immature, disobedient and selfish group of people together while calling them a church family. When you're the only pastoral leader, the example and the one that must set the standard, it's very hard. If you're among a small group of elders or deacons who are trying to carry the load of holiness for the entire church, no doubt you're tired. You're attempting to hold up a 5 pillar temple with only one pillar. If this is the case for you, then you undoubtedly feel the weight of your ministry.

Drawing by Missionary Brian Tressler

Imagine a single pastor carrying the entire weight of the city, the church the entire vision upon his "lone" shoulders. This reminds me of the old Atlas statue that has the weight of the entire world upon his back. This weight belongs on the back of only one person, the Lord Jesus Christ.

There is a more excellent way, thank God!

Mat 11:29 - 30 Take my yoke upon you, and learn of me; for I am meek and lowly in heart: and ye shall find rest unto your souls. For my yoke is easy, and my burden is light.

The New Testament government ministry load should be held up by five pillar giftings that are well able to hold up the weight of the ministry. *(This type and shadow is represented by God's 5 fold grace gifting and the 5 pillars of the entrance of the tabernacle's holy place.)* Think about all of the ministries today that are being held up by one lone pastor who must hold up the entire ministry on their own. Remember how God purposed that the ark of His presence was to be carried on the shoulders of multiple priests, and never by one man or a man made cart ministry. God struck down Uzzah who put his hand upon the ark to correct it during the stumbling of the oxen and the shifting of the cart in King David's day. Uzzah crossed the holy line and came into direct contact with God's power, and his house was "burned down" because the ministry was wired wrong. This is the danger of the "cart ministry".

I heard a minister who once said, "You will know when you have a cart ministry on your hands, because a cart ministry is made of "Boards" and "Big Wheels".

A Well Rounded Meal For The People

There are 5 major food groups that a person needs every day to stay healthy.
1. Fats, Oils & Sweets
2. Milk, Yogurt & Cheese
3. Meat, Poultry, Fish, Beans, Eggs, Nuts, Vegetables
4. Fruits
5. Breads, Cereal, Rice Pasta

There's also 5 *ministry* food groups that Christians need in their lives to stay healthy. These five ministry gifts are essential to the spiritual diet of a believer (*Eph 4:11 – 16*). The scripture indicates that these five ministry food groups will build, perfect, strengthen and mature a believer.

1. Apostles
2. Prophets
3. Evangelists
4. Pastors
5. Teachers

31

If I only eat chicken for an extended time, my body is going to become sick. If I just eat bread I'll become malnourished. In the same way, any Christian who's only eating from one gift is malnourished and unable to reach maturity and perfection.

Today's church world is very malnourished. Many churches function with only one of the five spiritual food groups. Can you guess which one? It's the pastor. Every church has a pastor, but how many churches do you know that have a prophet, an evangelist or an apostle on staff. We simply have not made room for these gifts through ignorance and *"corporation styled governing"*.

Why are we so heavily lopsided with pastoral/shepherd ministry? You might be surprised at the answer – coming in a moment.

True shepherds hang around with sheep, they watch over and care for the sheep. A well balanced 5 fold ministry will take on the true ministry of Jesus Christ as the great shepherd.

You and I are sheep if we are called into Christ's fold. However we are also a lot more than just sheep. We are ambassadors for Christ, we are more than conquerors through Him, a royal priesthood, a holy nation, and we are the violent that take the Kingdom by force. We are a royal priesthood and we are kings according to the bible. However, these are not qualities that are found in sheep.

The Old Testament type and shadow patterns of Moses' tabernacle show that the priests had to enter the holy place daily by stepping through the 5 fold pillars of grace. In this holy place, the priests would minister before God by caring for the candlestick (the Word), the table of shew bread (the body) and the altar of incense (the worship). For lack of space we can only scratch the surface of the tabernacle study, and I recommend that you spend quality time in this rich place of study. Our web-site has a list of resources and suggested authors that address this topic. Go to www.basicsforsuccess.com .

When a church or ministry is dominant only in the shepherd/pastoral gifting, the people will be as sheep. Sheep are skittish, fearful, dumb and easily spooked. They're afraid of their own shadow, and they only do two things for the shepherd:

1. They reproduce more sheep.
2. They produce wool for the shepherd to shear/fleece.

However, a pastoral based church and sheep are weak because they don't have the other God-appointed giftings maturing them *(Eph. 4:11 – 16)* as ambassadors, overcomers, saints, kings, priests and forcefully advancing Christian evangelists. Try to tell two people with a sheep mentality to leave the sheep fold, head over that mountain and establish a work for Christ. Those two sheep will tell you, *"Baaaaad maaaaaan!"*.

Today's pastoral based ministries are heavy in raising sheep. However, many of these sheep (and some pastors) wouldn't know an apostle if he was standing in their midst. Pastors aren't capable alone of training up the saints to be mature and raising the fullness of the stature of Christ. No single gifting is capable. They are also not eligible to escape every wind of doctrine that comes to lead them astray because they don't have a prophet on hand to point out the pitfalls of satanic "angel of light" doctrines. If you've pastored for only a short period of time, then you've probably already stumbled in areas that a prophet could have saved you from.

1 Cor 12:28 And God hath set some in the church, first apostles, secondarily prophets, thirdly teachers, after that miracles, then gifts of healings, helps, governments, diversities of tongues.

God sets the order in the church with apostles being first. Notice that the pastor is not even mentioned in this scripture. If this New Testament governmental scripture is giving the order of God for the church, why do we have a pastor leading virtually every church in the land in this century? The pastor was mentioned towards the end in the divine order of Eph. 4:11, and not mentioned at all in I Cor. 12:28. Beloved, we're out of balance and divine order.

I have been a pastor. If you are currently a pastor, I want you to know that I am not at all bashing or crashing into your territory or demeaning your holy position in God's ministry. I have felt your pain and suffering, and I've been under the heavy load of pastoral based ministry. I have also been on the other side, and I'm telling you that the grass is greener over here! I am trying to deliver you from unwarranted weight and false responsibility that is not yours, which you were never meant to carry. Taking a fresh look at the scriptures and your responsibilities as a pastor will set you free and lift your burden. Remember, I don't intend to offend you, but I only have a desire to see you free and liberated with your house wired correctly.

Let's look at history in brief. The pastoral based ministry comes from a long history of man-filtered religion. Starting with the Roman Catholic Church and the papacy, generations have followed a papal church model which has a single man as the head of the church. The "Vicar of Christ" or the Pope is the central figure of the Roman Catholic Church. He and his words are supposedly infallible according to Roman Catholic dogma, and anyone who challenges his words should be put to death. He is the presiding official of God's government on earth according to the Roman Catholic church.

Through this long standing man-made religious model, we have created traditional "old time" church governments which consist of the simple "corporation styled" governing model. We have the pastor/pope/president who is the head of the corporation/body. We have the associate pastor/vice president who's second in command. We then have a church board of elders or deacons who act as the board of directors who make the governing decisions of the church/corporation. These board members are typically voted in by the people of the church/the

34

investors, and must perform somewhat similar to a political official to keep their place of authority and stature. This is no different than the American corporate dream, and our church governments are formed around man's idea of ruling corporate vision. You will never find in Old Testament pattern or New Testament scriptures, a recipe for these types of governments in God's ministry.

MINISTRY	CORPORATION
Pastor/Pope	President
Associate Pastor	Vice President
Elder or Deacon Board	Board of Directors
Treasurer	Treasurer
Voting Congregation	Investors/Stockholders

For years we've done a pretty good job of running things, as we've gotten some nice buildings, some great things going in our cities, and we've got typical corporate church growth just like the stock market. On a good year, we can boast 10 – 20% church growth, and on a bad year where we dropped 5%, we're ready to vote out or fire the officers or board of directors. We've even authorized and trained the sheep to think this way, and we've given them voting power to choose their destiny, their leaders and their message that the leaders will preach. Immature sheep with full voting power to decide their diets will gain unto themselves teachers who will speak what their itching ears want to hear. They will play their own little form of "Let's hire a president", and they'll do it in God's holy church. It's no different than allowing your 5 year old child to decide what he/she wants to eat for each meal. We all know that candy bars and ice cream won't grow them to maturity and health.

God's Kingdom is not a democracy. It never has been, and it never will be. God's Kingdom is a theocracy. I like what one man of God said, "Being a part of a theocracy government means that you have the right to sit down and shut up. God runs this kingdom. He's the King, and you're not". King David had the true heart when he said:

The Business Of Ministry

Psa 84:10 For a day in thy courts is better than a thousand. I had rather be a doorkeeper in the house of my God, than to dwell in the tents of wickedness.

We must be content to be doorkeepers and servants in His house, rather than a ruler in our own house of sin *(mark missing)*.

God doesn't allow the sheep to vote their leaders into His church. The people fell into great sin in Saul's day when they demanded a king so they could be like the other political nations. God gave them their political king, and he lost the kingdom on the first assignment due to his political nature. God's men aren't voted in, they're *"SET, PLACED AND APPOINTED"* by God.

1 Cor 12:28 And God hath set some in the church, first apostles, secondarily prophets, thirdly teachers . .

Any man or woman that is voted into a corporate, pastoral based church will have to keep performing the same stunts and jumping through the same hoops to stay in that church. They voted you in and they can definitely vote you out! Remember, sheep vote because they like you, not because you're speaking for God. Remember also that sheep don't have the ability to know right from wrong on their own. Ask any natural shepherd. Sheep can't even sense evil if it was ready to pounce on them from above. They'll follow one another right off a cliff if given an opportunity. What are we leaders doing, allowing them to vote on who's going to lead them? What about God's decision? This is a disastrous mixture that could lead to the rebellion as of Korah *(Num. 16)* against the true men of God.

Remember that God's men were always hated and killed by their very own. God's prophets spoke pure words of intense light and deliverance, and those words usually bought them a deliverance ticket straight to Heaven at an early age.

Luke 13:34 O Jerusalem, Jerusalem, which killest the prophets, and stonest them that are sent unto thee; how often would I have gathered thy children together, as a hen doth gather her brood under her wings, and ye would not!

Nowhere in the bible is there ever a corporation based government set up by God. It's simply not his M.O. *(Method of operation).* His government is a kingdom government. His government is established on the number of grace (5) with first apostles, prophets, evangelists, pastors and teachers. This 5 fold government gifting is the gift of God. It makes ministry easy once again, and it causes the people of God to mature and grow up into the fullness of Christ's stature. The five fold ministry equals the five fingered "hand of God" upon the people of God.

Rev 1:17 And when I saw him, I fell at his feet as dead. And he laid his right hand upon me, saying unto me, Fear not; I am the first and the last:

Under the glorious presence of Jesus Christ, the apostle John couldn't stand, but he fell as a dead man in Christ's presence. However the five fingered right hand of Jesus upon John caused him to be able to stand, to write and to proceed in Spirit-led ministry. He saw a white haired (matured) Jesus with passionate fire in His eyes, feet burning with destiny and a sharp sword coming from His mouth. This is what the matured body of Christ will look like under the 5 fold hand of Christ's ministry!

Throughout history the right hand of a king was the hand of authority, power and decree. When he held his scepter with his right hand, whatever he decreed was done. This is the same with the five fingered hand of God through His 5 New Testament fold ministry on the earth today.

The five fold ministry also equals the 5 pillars at the entrance of the holy place at the tabernacle of Moses. Only priests could enter into this area to minister before the Lord. The grace and government of God is the secret heavenly power which activates a royal priesthood who will minister before the Lord day and night.

37

Why would we want to set up the ministry government any other way than under God's New Testament command? We once were ignorant, but now God is bringing us into accountability so that He can fill His church with His glorious manifest presence without harming the church and people. He is preparing a new wineskin that won't tear and lose the wine *(Lu. 5:37 – 39)*.

Some may say, "Well then the entire church is out of focus and is out of order! How can this be, and why hasn't God stepped in to change this?" I've spoken to many people who get angry when they think of the governmental imperfection in the church. However, we have to remember that God is changing and cleansing His church to present her Holy and acceptable. He's bringing her forward from glory to glory. Thank God that He has brought us forward, past the Roman Catholic heresies to Luther's reform where Martin nailed the decrees to the Roman Catholic church door and separated himself from papal based government, calling the pope the anti-Christ. We've come far past the fiery Methodists, the Wesleyan movement, the Pentecostal movement, the healing movement, the Word of faith movement, and the prophetic movement. God is now bringing us to the apostolic movement as He is restoring His governmental order to the church of Jesus Christ. Churches, leaders and pastors everywhere are responding to the Word of the Lord and are bailing out of their "old wineskins" in pursuit of the "new wineskin" that will hold the new wine. They're going in their joy and selling everything they've ever had and ever been about, and purchasing the new field because of the treasure that they've found hidden in that field.

The parables of the hidden treasure, the pearl of great price, the net cast into the sea, and the householder all speak the same hidden thing.

Mat 13:44 Again, the kingdom of heaven is like unto treasure hid in a field; the which when a man hath found, he hideth, and for joy thereof goeth and selleth all that he hath, and buyeth that field.

38

Many burned out, frustrated and aggravated leaders are responding to God's call all over the world and are re-wiring their ministries in preparation for God to throw the switch and ignite the house of God with Heaven's power.

Many others are submitting under the mighty hand of God and are renewing their old wine skins by unlacing them, allowing them to dry out under the heat of the sun, allowing the Master to rub fresh anointing oil throughout their leather ministry with great pressure. They're becoming flexible again and willing to take on any new shape that God would require. Their new structure is able to handle the pressure of the new wine. They're being laced back up (in God's time) and prepared for a fresh infilling of God's destiny and purpose.

Can you hear God calling you to rewire your ministry?

Many men and women of God are beginning to learn who they really are in the mind of God. Many prophets are struggling with little churches because of their prophetic black and white messages that only attracts other prophets and those giftings. They're realizing that they are playing the role of a pastor, but they're really not a pastor. A prophet doesn't make a very good "pastoral based" church leader! If he or she is honest, he will even tell you that.

Evangelists are realizing that they've been standing as pastors when really their hearts are to reach the world for Christ. Every Sunday the same salvation message proceeds from them in one of a thousand different ways, and the saved sheep are starving because they're only getting one of the 5 spiritual food groups week after week, the baby's milk of new birth.

Apostles are realizing that they've been fulfilling the pastoral role because that's the only paying, salaried position in the church. They're men and women of great vision and authority, but their vision is stifled and hindered every day because of the overload of local pastoral duties that they must single-handedly bear up.

An immature pastor/teacher could become intimidated by this message and by the other giftings, unless he is confident and secure in the position that God has placed him in. It's quite a shock to a pastor *(or any single ministry gifting)* for him to suddenly find out that he must bring the other offices in with authority. It can be a great blow to the ego of man to find out that God isn't depending on just you and your gift alone, but that you're only 1/5 of God's total governmental plan for the church. He has other gifts that you don't operate in and He wants to use them also to build His church. This calls for true humility and self abasement in order for a true pastor/teacher to turn his old wineskin church model into a new wineskin that will qualify for the future power of God's next apostolic movement.

Only ego and pride will stop a church from the most excellent way.

When the power switch is thrown in this next "new wine" movement, the glory of God will be weighty and the signs, wonders and miracles will be too numerous to number. The growth of the church will be exponential rather than corporate based percentage growth. Ask a pastor of a pastoral based ministry if he or she is ready for a 6 night per week revival for the rest of their lives and you will get a lot of various answers. The current weight of the ministry is too heavy for this man of God to carry alone, and he's under tremendous political and man-made stress to outperform the other local organizations on the heavenly stock market. He's trying to figure out how to grow 10% this year and keep his job. Tell him that he has the capacity to double in size in one month and you will find many pastors who don't want this growth and commitment. They simply can't bear the burden of that kind of growth, knowing the weight of counseling, building size problems, contentions and flesh that he'll have to deal with. However, give the pastor 4 other ministry gifts to stand alongside in unity and agreement, and that pastor will be ready to spring into action!

THE SET MAN

I must make one thing very clear. There must be true authority set in the church before God throws the power switch. However, it's understood that there's always a leader among leaders. There's a SET MAN in every house, as God has SET these gifts...

*1 Cor 12:28 And God hath **set** some in the church, first apostles, secondarily prophets, thirdly teachers, after that miracles, then gifts of healings, helps, governments, diversities of tongues.*

Anything with two or more heads is a monster. I'm not trying to say that the body of Christ is a five headed being. However, I am saying that the five fold ministry giftings will successfully grow you up into the head which is Christ. Jesus walked in a powerful anointing as an apostle, a prophet, an evangelist and pastor/teacher. He was all five of these gifts wrapped up into one ministry. However, I've personally never met a person who "IS" all five of these gifts. It is certainly probable that an apostle will operate in all five of these gifts as needed, especially when taking new territory and starting churches. Apostles don't operate in all five gifts at once, as they need the other gifts alongside of them to ease the burden and create the hand of God in their ministry.

A SET MAN can be any one of the five fold giftings. God may set a pastor as the head of a church. James was the set man of the church in Jerusalem. Once the brethren had counseled together, Pastor James stood and gave the final word on the matter.

Acts 15:13 And after they had held their peace, James answered, saying, Men and brethren, hearken unto me:

41

Are you the "Set Man" of the house? Are you the God ordained leader of the church or ministry that you're standing in and serving? If not, then find the set man and offer your submission and help. If you are, then lead with the authority given to you by God.

HOW DO I KNOW IF I'M THE SET MAN?

If you are the one with the God breathed vision for the house that you're in, and if you have the grace upon you to lead the people that are with you, then you're most likely the "Set Man". God ordains and anoints the leader as He sees fit. Corporate fasting and prayer will always reveal who the "Set Man" is. If you are unsure, get the leaders of the ministry to fast and pray. God will speak clearly to everyone.

When God sets a man or woman over a house, there is no one who should vote him out. God set him there. He's there under divine Kingdom order. No man can legally interfere with God's choosing and God's decision. Remember, we serve in a theocracy, and that means, *"God is the boss and we are the servants".*

When God sets a man or a husband/wife as the SET MAN of the house, the other apostolic five fold giftings that come alongside of him/her must come in submission to the SET MAN. This requires a heart of submission to authority, a willingness to give way to the set man's final say, and an absolute trust in God as the ruler of the house and as the one capable of directing the set man. Likewise, great humility and servant hood must be the lifestyle and character of the set man, as he/she will have to give way and heed to the counsel of the other five fold giftings when they have a word from the Lord. There's no place for pride and arrogance in the shoes of the set man. Likewise, a five fold government ministry must be submitted to one another and to the Lord's purpose.

Of course, if there were blatant sin issues in a member of the five fold ministry team, the five fold ministry team would exercise complete authority, even if it meant removing the set man of the house. Submission to the set man does not include submitting to a sinful or arrogant lifestyle in God's holy church.

Phil 2:3 - 8 Let nothing be done through strife or vainglory; but in lowliness of mind let each esteem other better than themselves. Look not every man on his own things, but every man also on the things of others. Let this mind be in you, which was also in Christ Jesus: Let nothing be done through strife or vainglory; but in lowliness of mind let each esteem other better than themselves. Look not every man on his own things, but every man also on the things of others. Let this mind be in you, which was also in Christ Jesus: Who, being in the form of God, thought it not robbery to be equal with God: But made himself of no reputation, and took upon him the form of a servant, and was made in the likeness of men: And being found in fashion as a man, he humbled himself, and became obedient unto death, even the death of the cross.

I love the story that a man told during a pastor's conference years ago. It impacted my life as I heard him tell the conference crowd that he has surrounded himself with men who love Jesus more than he does, and that he submits himself to these men and their direction.   He said that if he thought God had spoken to him with direction for himself or the church, and after presenting it to these men that he's submitted to, if they feel that he's deceived or they don't feel like that was the Lord was speaking, he will consider himself deceived and will forsake the direction. What a notable and safe place to live! God speaks through the mouths of two or three witnesses, and He will speak wisdom when you have the spirit of submission to authority and the character of servant hood among those whom you've surrounded yourself with.

Prov 11:14 Where no counsel is, the people fall: but in the multitude of counselors there is safety.

43

FIVE FOLD MINISTRY CHARACTERISTICS

The five fold ministry working together will always exemplify the full counsel of God's grace on the earth. The fullness of Christ is displayed through the direction, drive and giftings of the five fold ministry.

Apostle – (sent one) This gifting frequently displays a vision for great things, much greater than humanly possible. An apostle has been sent by God to plow new territories, to release creative power and to activate the gifts of God within His people. His vision commonly reaches farther than anyone that he's working with, and can include a vision for an entire city, a state, nation or the nations of the world. An apostle's vision is ever increasing and growing as he takes more ground for the Kingdom of God. Demons and high principalities are commonly submitted to the anointing of an apostle who's been sent by God into their area, and they will move at his command. An apostle can typically operate in any and all of the five fold giftings as he moves in and out of "called to" areas. He won't always focus upon them all, but has liberty to move in the five giftings and to release others to move in their giftings. An apostle is a foundation builder.

The apostle is an ambassador for the Kingdom of Heaven and he speaks for Heaven. Many signs, wonders and miracles take place when an apostle is operating in his functional gift. Creativity explodes and people are supernaturally changed and activated through the words of the apostle. Woe to any future church that doesn't have an apostle to train them in ambassadorship. The anti-apostolic message that's rampant in the church is one of *"This is not my home, I'm just passing through"*. That message will keep the saints immature, non-productive and homeless!

Prophet - A prophet is a seer, one with insight and understanding of the times, seasons, tactics of the enemy and the best spiritual C.I.A. operative that a ministry can have. A prophet is shown hidden things by God who uncovers them to the prophet. The mature prophet knows how to receive and give out tactical Kingdom information, and he/she knows how to intercede when the information comes. The prophet knows how to handle unbelief when other leaders don't see things the way that God has shown them to the prophet. The mature prophet has learned to deal with unbelief, criticism and shunning from other leaders and Christians, and doesn't take these attitudes personally. The prophet must understand that God's people have always stoned and silenced the prophets, and that their duty before God is a holy and awesome duty that is misunderstood by many.

Prophets are also announcers and declarers of the Word of the Lord. They have the increased supernatural ability to "decree a thing" under Holy Ghost inspiration and it will come to pass. When God gets ready to do something divine in the earth, He first tells his prophets.

Amos 3:7 Surely the Lord GOD will do nothing, but he revealeth his secret unto his servants the prophets.

Woe to the future church who has not a prophet! Woe to the church that has a prophet and refuses to listen to his words!

Evangelist – The evangelist's duty typically is to remind the saints of their evangelistic duty, to train them up as evangelists, and to creatively invent new and innovative ways to communicate the gospel of Jesus Christ to the masses. The "old school" evangelist used to go from church to church and hold revival meetings, where the people would bring their unsaved ones to hear the presentation of the evangelist. Once the evangelist left, so did the evangelism message. The saints were not trained up in evangelism, and they didn't continue the working of the message of salvation in their community. This is not who the evangelist is.

The evangelist's duty is to train saints to be evangelists and breakers, taking the kingdom by force and occupying their God

45

given territory for Jesus Christ, sweeping in the souls of men around them. The evangelist will make evangelists out of all Christian people who have ears to hear and hearts to learn, obey and grow.

Typically, today's sheep don't evangelize. However, they are created to. Sheep are supposed to reproduce sheep and wool. The evangelist will stir up the gifts of God within a believer so that the heart of God for the lost can be transplanted into the believer. With this heart transplant, the believer will be able to experience a flow of the agape love of God which flows to all people, rich, poor, great, small, criminal, ugly and homeless. This is the place where miracles flow, supernatural provision takes place, and hearts are changed. Woe to any future church who doesn't have an evangelist on board to build up the saints to become evangelists.

Pastor/Teacher (Shepherd) – The Pastor/teacher is the one who loves the sheep and wants to be near them. He wants to be close to them and is concerned about their every day issues of life. A pastor loves to sit with them in the hospital, to consul them and to drink tea with them at their homes when they're having a bad day. The pastor is able to check the sheep for parasites, and can determine if they're drinking bad water or eating poisoned food. The pastor is able to direct the sheep so they don't go off course, and the sheep know his voice – they're dear and close to him. The pastor is typically a teacher of the Word of God, and is able to break the word down into day by day instruction so the people of God know how to live, walk and be successful in life. The teaching gift normally loves to break down the Word into Greek and Hebrew meanings, and the teacher loves to spend hours upon hours developing applicable teachings that will help the people of God to live in the victory of God's covenant.

Teacher: Most pastors are also teachers, but not all teachers are pastors. Therefore, you will find that the teacher gift has the same qualities mentioned above concerning the keen ability to teach the Word of God in a relevant way that help people to live in victory.

We're not talking about traditional church order here. The gifts of the five fold ministry represent the entire counsel of God's grace through Jesus Christ. With them all in operation together, you get full counsel and fullness of the stature of Christ.

I've heard church people complain who fully understand the five fold ministry. They can't understand why their apostle won't come to the hospital and sit with them all day while they recover from a hangnail. They think that he's a heartless pastor, but he's really an apostle. They don't understand why a prophet won't come and listen to their woes and problems without bringing biblical correction to them for their attitude and unbelief. They don't understand that they're calling on the wrong gifts. They need the pastoral gift and there's grace for the pastor to operate in this gift. When you're dying in the hospital, that's when you need an apostle or prophet who will come and raise you up with a distinct miracle or word from Heaven. Don't call on an apostle or prophet if you just want to have tea and crumpets and talk about how you're feeling lately. They don't have the grace to operate as a pastor, unless the apostle is breaking new territory and there's a need for pastoral operation and the pastor has not yet arrived on the scene.

Now that you understand the general direction of these ministry giftings, attempt to find out where you belong. Then pray and ask God how to develop your ministry government under the five fold ministry anointing.

It's quite possible that a small ministry may not have all five gifts operating within it. That's alright. Develop relationships with covenant brothers that you trust who will come and impart their gifts into your people from time to time, so that they can get a balanced spiritual diet from the full counsel of God.

The Business Of Ministry

Luke 5:37 - 39 And no man putteth new wine into old bottles; else the new wine will burst the bottles, and be spilled, and the bottles shall perish. But new wine must be put into new bottles; and both are preserved. No man also having drunk old wine straightway desireth new: for he saith, The old is better.

Pastoral based ministries are the old wineskin. Don't waste your time developing another one of these. There's already plenty of them today and God doesn't need another one. Develop your ministry as a five fold apostolic ministry so that you can be in divine New Testament order when God throws the power switch in your ministry. The new wineskin is the way of the 21st century church, and one that God will gloriously fill with the power of His presence. If you want divine exponential increase, build according to the New Testament plan that God has commanded.

*Eph 2:19, 20 NIV Consequently, you are no longer foreigners and aliens, but fellow citizens with God's people and members of God's household, **built on the foundation of the apostles and prophets,** with Christ Jesus himself as the chief cornerstone.*

*Eph 4:1 - 131 NIV **It was he who gave some to be apostles, some to be prophets, some to be evangelists, and some to be pastors and teachers,** to prepare God's people for works of service, so that the body of Christ may be built up, until we all reach unity in the faith and in the knowledge of the Son of God and become mature, attaining to the whole measure of the fullness of Christ.*

ESTABLISHING YOUR MINISTRY
U.S. NON-PROFIT ORGANIZATION OR NOT?
(U.S. BASED MINISTRIES)

When establishing the business of your ministry, you must decide whether or not you want to incorporate and become a non-profit 501(C)3 organization. You have two options:

1. File paperwork with your Secretary of State's office and start a non profit corporation which can then apply for federal tax exemption with the IRS.
2. Operate your ministry as a church which does not recognize IRS tax exemption or state corporation status. Your activities (if you are a church) are tax exempt under separation of church and state laws.

There are upsides and downsides to each of these decisions. I'll attempt to give a brief overview of a few of them.

If you choose to start a corporation with the State that you reside in, you enter into a submissive contract with the state government. You must then from that point onward, perform the business of your ministry under some direction and scrutiny of the state. You must always have a board of directors and corporate officers. These officers and directors will be held legally accountable for every financial and active decision made by the corporation. If your ministry is a five-fold one, put the five-fold ministers as directors and elect officers from among them.

Many people believe that being a corporation separates you from personal liability, however the opposite is true. If the corporation ever owes taxes, fees or penalties, these can be directly assessed to each officer and director until paid in full. Collection proceedings can take place against you personally with liens filed against your person, your home, your personal property, etc. If the corporation breaks any state or federal law, knowingly or unknowingly, any and all directors can be charged and imprisoned as part of the penalty for breaking the law.

Most of these things will never happen, and are seldom, if ever heard of. However, the state does retain the right to step in to your ministry and do just about whatever they want to do. They can audit your books, look into your board meeting minutes and ask as many questions as they wish. The principle of the matter is that the state becomes an authority over your ministry when your non-profit organization is submitted for approval through the state corporation process.

Most ministries operate within the normal laws of the land and they don't have a problem with submitting to normal corporate state and business procedures. They understand that a good attorney can stop or slow down any encroachment of the state if there were unnecessary actions being taken. They don't have a problem with making annual reports to the state and disclosing the board of directors and/or the officers of the corporation. They also don't have a problem paying the annual fee to file their annual state paperwork. They plan to operate by the book and therefore have no plans of controversy with the state.

They also understand that the corporation *(if filed as a non-profit)* is no longer privately held. There is no individual profit gained from any person or persons on the board of directors, officers or employees/members. The non-profit tax status is given by the state and the IRS because no individual is profiting from the financial directives of the organization. This doesn't mean that people can't receive salaries for performance. However, you would be scrutinized as you grow if the pastor or leader of the church took 10% of the tithes and offerings received as a salary. This would be profiting off of the growth and increase of the organization the same as a sales commission, and would be generally thought of as a violation of your non-profit status.

The Business Of Ministry

If you set up your state corporation as a non-profit organization, this only means that the state recognizes you as non-profit. Some states require further proof of your non-profit status before they will allow you to be exempt from sales, use and property taxes. Some states will require that you are also considered non-profit by the IRS. This is another step in the process. As of this writing, the IRS charges a $500 fee for you to apply for non profit recognition. The forms are long and tedious and unless you know what you are doing, you need to get some help from a seasoned professional or attorney firm. If you don't fill out the paperwork correctly, send it in correctly, add all supporting evidence and documents, and a host of other pertinent secrets, your determination by the IRS could take up to 5 years for approval. My first non-profit organization application was applied for in 1980 and we didn't receive a final determination from the IRS until 1983. I've heard of many 5 year horror stories since then. However, over the years we've learned what the IRS wants and how they think, and have helped multiple ministries to get their determination letters in 45 – 60 days or shortly thereafter. This is considered a modern day miracle in this day and age. Thanks be to God!

Once you have IRS 501(c)3 status because they have sent you the "all important" determination letter, you will have everything you need to prove that your organization is tax-exempt *"within the purposes of your organization"*. As far as most Americans and the laws of the federal and state government are concerned, you're now "officially non-profit".

As far as God is concerned, you're "official" when He says you're official. Official standing with God is called a divine calling from Heaven.

If you choose not to have your ministry become a corporation and decide to operate as a church under the separation of church/state laws, you may be able to operate successfully in this manner. However, you must be prepared to give an answer every day for your decision. Many Americans are so deeply brain washed, submersed and generally "pickled" with state control that they will look at a separated "church" ministry which has chosen not to have state and federal acknowledgement as a separatist radical para-military group that they need to avoid like the plague. They will wonder why you won't submit to the governing authorities or subject yourself to the same criteria as "all the rest of them". You will find yourself being questioned repeatedly by people who are trying to figure out your stand and position. Many will not feel comfortable giving to your ministry because they are almost sure that their donations are not tax-exempt with the IRS. Many people are so hopelessly locked into the system that they can't imagine working with someone who's unplugged. Therefore, this is a moral and conviction issue that you will need to pray about and decide upon. You need to study to show yourself approved and find wisdom from others who have made the same decision as the one you're considering.

As of this writing, our ministry is recognized as a 501(c)3 non-profit, state-authorized corporation. We chose this because we don't have the personal time and we're not called to spend our focused energy and time educating Christians on this issue. This is our conviction. Everyone must choose their battles, and this is one that is not ours at this time. We don't have a problem with having records available to the public or to the state and the IRS. As a matter of fact, we're heavily audited and scrutinized by an outside auditing firm so that we qualify for various grants and corporate funding. We don't mind having a board of directors and officers who will direct the organization, however we do understand apostolic five fold ministry in the New Testament church, and the board of directors and officers are all understanding of the five fold apostolic team, and they're submitted to one another for accountability. We don't mind having a "required" annual board meeting because we have directors meetings monthly or quarterly anyway. I'm sure that any organization that doesn't meet at least once per year is probably not one that's really doing anything as an organization anyway. We have chosen to keep a tight control on our organization so we don't personally end up in jail because of the actions of one another. We have opted to pay the annual registration fee with the state for corporate filing. We do this because we don't want to bring unnecessary offense to people that we're trying to reach. We know that the devil's schemes are rampant in the earth today and we don't want the corporate issue to be an unnecessary stumbling block of offense against people who need Jesus. Therefore, they can rest in the fact that we're organized and registered with the state, we're current with our IRS form 990 and supporting attachments, we're audited regularly and all of their donations are tax deductible. This is our conviction, and you have the right to yours.

As far as my personal heart, I don't depend on any state or federal government to license my ministry or our church and apostolic functions. I must serve God rather than men.

Acts 5:29 Then Peter and the other apostles answered and said, We ought to obey God rather than men.

I know that if all of the corporate paperwork and business was taken away tomorrow, I still have the same ministry that God gave to me when He called me. When I give, I could really care less if my gifts are tax deductible. I give where God tells me to give, and most of my giving doesn't get recorded for my tax records anyway. I'm not living inside the box of worldly thinking and the need for tax deductions. I also teach those around me to do the same and live outside of the traditional corporate mentality.

I also understand that I am somewhat liable for the actions of our board and officers, and for the purpose and direction of the corporation. I could end up in jail or charged with a crime if my co-partners decide to do something stupid. However, that's the risk that I personally am willing to take, because I have surrounded myself with people of great honor and trust.

Lastly, I want to make it clear that it's important for God's ministers to be prepared at any time to turn in your state and federal paperwork, if EVER the state steps in and begins to control the church, the ministry and the functions of God upon this earth. I stand ready to withdraw from the state and federal corporate system if the government ever commands our ministry to:

1. Hire homosexuals or non-believers into our holy ministry as an act of so called equal rights.
2. Command our organization to keep the gospel of Jesus Christ within the 4 walls of our building, denying our freedom of speech in the open markets, streets and places of public assembly.
3. Exact fines, imprisonment, fees or taxes upon us for obeying the scriptures or crossing our freedom of religion.
4. Any other encroachment or penalty exacted upon us as a corporation because of our religious stand for the Word of God.

We live in the greatest free nation on the earth! I am very patriotic towards this great land and our God-given constitution. However, there have been issues on the table in our congress in recent years that have threatened the removal of our religious and constitutional freedoms. Thank God that these movements have been stifled in the past. However, the next generation coming might not be so fortunate as darkness attempts to creep in among our legislators, presidents and judges. One of the most critical decisions you may have to make is to renounce, turn in, annul and dissolve your corporation as a holy stand against the "lawless law" of government encroachment. Let's pray that in this nation we will never see that day come upon us as it has in so many nations around the world.

HELP IS AVAILABLE: If you would like our consortium group to help you with your state and federal application paperwork, you can find these resources at www.basicsforsucces.com.

If you want to establish a bank account for your ministry, you will be required to either have a registered corporation name or a registered business name with the Secretary of State's office. If you decide not to incorporate and want to just call your ministry the XYZ Church, then you will need to go to the Secretary of State's office in your state and register this name as a fictitious entity under your social security number, allowing them to check to see if that name is already in use in their state. They will ask you for your personal information so that anyone who attempts to find out about the XYZ Church will be directed by the Secretary of State's office to your name, physical address and phone number. Showing this state registered business paperwork is the only way to get a checking account in the XYZ Church name in America.

It's unfortunate but true that the noose of government registration, licensing laws and financial tracking is closing around the necks of everyone great and small in this nation. All ministers would be wise to study your constitutional rights while making a stand to preserve them, stay active in understanding the making of laws in your land, inform your people of political stands and encourage voting among your people. Our nation needs the holy ministry of God to stand for righteousness, liberty and freedom at all costs, especially in the coming days.

BUSINESS AND LEGAL PAPERWORK:

Every business and ministry must have adequate paperwork. Some of it is required by law, and other paperwork is required by God. God is one of decency and order, and there's nothing worse than a ministry with it's paperwork out of order. Disarray is not one of the fruits of the Holy Spirit, and God is not the author of confusion. He's not impressed with our *"box of receipts"* theology.

When I was just starting in ministry I used to be horrible at bookkeeping. I don't know how this happened, but while I starting in youth ministry, I still couldn't reconcile a checkbook.

I guess it was a glitch in my person, and was certainly an area of weakness that the devil would attack over and over. I would bounce checks as if I was trying to, and I would always pay the price for it in more ways than I could imagine. My bank wouldn't loan me money because they could see that I was no good with the money I had. My friends wouldn't trust my check because they'd all heard of my character failures with previously bounced checks. The "bad check" companies all knew my name when the store clerk did an electronic check approval *(it's not good to be on that mailing list)*. I had bills piled on my desk and I was always late in paying them, but not because I didn't have money. I was just unorganized and had no clue of how to get my paperwork in order. I hated the thought of taking time to write checks, lick stamps and write on envelopes.

This curse continued until I got myself in deep financial trouble and I was praying to God and blaming the devil. God spoke to me and sharply rebuked me for my disorder, confusion and lack of discipline. He also spoke the following words to me, *"If you're weak in an area, you must take authority and cover that area with strength."* In other words, He was telling me to go to school and learn how to balance my checkbook or hire an accountant to do it for me. I thought to myself, *"I can't afford school or an accountant."* However, I somehow could afford around $100 - $150 per month in bounced check charges and a scarred character reference.

I hired an accountant.

Our ministries are moving quickly these days. Before you know it we've finished another year. Get a calendar, an electronic reminder system, email calendar or Microsoft Outlook to remind you when it's time to:

1. Balance the checkbook each month.
2. Pay bills due on certain dates.
3. Have auto deductions and bill paying services activated.
4. Receive funds from those due on certain dates.

5. Review the previous month's activities and make a report of how to change and better yourself next year during that month.
6. When it's time to file your state and federal returns and other legal paperwork.
7. When it's time to have another board, group, staff or department meeting.
8. When birthdays, anniversaries and important events are coming up.

This is called the basics and beginning of strategic planning. With all of the gadgets and wonderful creative inventions that are available to us in this time that we live, there's no reason to ever be late, delinquent or forgetful ever again. Delinquency and failure is our own fault.

Taking authority over the time line calendar and commanding self discipline is the sign of a good child of God. This will build more character than you will ever know. It will also build God's trust in you. He's looking for those who are faithful in the little things before He starts handing over many cities to the faithful ones.

MINISTRY ACCOUNTABILITY
AUDITING OF YOUR BOOKS

As your ministry grows, you may want to have your ministry books professionally audited by an outside firm. Getting an outside auditor is beneficial for many reasons:
1. It shows accountability among your members and supporters.
2. It shows compliance with all laws and normal standards of operation.
3. It opens your ministry up to grant funding.
4. It gives you greater authority for opened doors in your city and region.

If you plan on tapping into future governmental, corporate or estate funds or grants, then an annual audit is absolutely required. We have found an annual audit to be most beneficial for these very reasons. When companies, state agencies or organizations ask you for financial information it is nice to be able to throw them a professional, annual audited statement of your ministry. This carries a lot of weight and stops a lot of unnecessary red tape that you'd otherwise have to go through. I know of many ministries who refuse to come up into the excellence of an audit, and they wonder why the doors keep shutting to them when they apply for grants or attempt to get corporations, larger ministries and governments to work with them in their programs.

You will find that audits are standard requirements for any organization or ministry that wants to request grant funding from corporations or governmental agencies. Without an audited financial statement, you won't get very far with grant funding, so be prepared to do this before filling out your first grant request.

Our ministry used to be under a local spirit of skepticism and accusation along with all ministries in town due to the religious and fearful spirit that presided in our city. Although I never touched or counted the offerings, I didn't write the checks for the bills, and I had built every possible device of protection for the ministry's finances, there were still floating accusations that would harass us and other ministries from time to time. We'd hear of some disgruntled church member or an outside accuser who took a shot at us in the area of finances. This all stopped once we were professionally audited. The auditors checked our accounting, our claims and our financial procedures. They searched for every penny and where it was placed throughout the year. Once they gave us a "two thumbs up" review, there was no place for accusation. This made the cost of the audit well worth our time and money. Our church members can rest at night knowing that their church organization doesn't have an embezzler or fraudulent person or persons handling the money.

We also found that we had greater access and ease in receiving licensing and permission with our city and county when it came to getting permission to do a fund raiser on a certain piece of property or a public outreach in a city park. Having a professional audited financial statement to include with any application that we submitted gave us legitimacy and a raised level of trust among other organizations. Simply put, a professional audited financial statement puts you in the same category as other organizations who understand the importance of the audit for their success and survival.

If you need help in finding a good professional auditor, you can find these resources at our web site www.basicsforsuccess.com .

Chapter 3 Review Points

- Educate yourself on New Testament apostolic ministry government.
- Discover what type of government your ministry operates under.
- Build a plan to renew your wineskin.
- Establish the "set man" order of your house.
- Find out which gifting you represent.
- Get the other giftings to your people to feed them a balanced spiritual meal.
- Decide whether or not to register as a non-profit.
- Get your ministry books in order.
- Consider having your ministry professionally audited.

The Business Of Ministry

Chapter Four
Principles And Guidelines

PROSPEROUS MULTI-GENERATIONAL INCREASE

Seeing the larger financial vision is vital to the health and prosperity of your ministry. You must consider that at some point you will need to hand off your ministry to someone who will take it farther than you ever could. Biblical examples would include Abraham and Isaac, Isaac and Jacob, Eli and Samuel, Moses and Joshua, Aaron and his sons, Elijah and Elisha, Jesus and the disciples.

Prov 13:22 A good man leaveth an inheritance to his children's children: and the wealth of the sinner is laid up for the just.

In proper vision casting, you must consider your spiritual grandchildren *(according to the scripture above)*. You'd better have some spiritual sons in the making, and they had better be making some spiritual sons as well. These are the ones that you must build for. When they become old enough to begin ministering in authority and power, will they have a blessing or a curse from spiritual granddad? Will they be given the same old tools that you had to work with or will they have more? Will they have to re-invent the wheel in ministry, or will they have impartation from you so that they can go farther with less trouble because of your experience and wisdom given freely to them?

Financially your ministry needs to be sound by the time your sons and grand sons take over. Just as you need to be saving 10% back from everything you do in your personal finances, so should your ministry be saving back 10% of everything that comes in (this is not the tithe). Saving 10% back for long term

61

investment is imperative for ministry health and prosperity. These saved funds are not available for paying monthly bills. They are investment dollars that will help future generations. They will continually increase, and by the third generation, will overtake that generation with great prosperity. These funds will buy lands and future buildings. They will be stored and invested for future use in the area of increase. Any good ministry organization worth it's salt will have long term, increasing reserves.

I remember what it was like having to make a large church building payment. I remember suffering in my personal finances because we needed to make that building payment so the church would have some place to meet. I paid that building payment for years by giving up my family's salary so the payment would be on time. Wouldn't it have been wonderful if a spiritual granddad would have made sure that we had the building payment covered by training my spiritual father and myself on how to build long term reserves? An inheritance of wisdom, knowledge and cash from a spiritual granddad would have been very helpful.

(Prov 13:22) A good man leaveth an inheritance to his children's children: and the wealth of the sinner is laid up for the just.

Don't continue the curse for your grandchildren. Get busy with passion and conviction, saving back 10% from every ministry dollar that comes. At the end of your ministry life, you will have retained 10% of everything earned, and you will have made it grow into great prosperity for your upcoming generations. You will have been a "Good Man" and will have left a generous inheritance for your spiritual and natural grandchildren.

This lifestyle of saving will in many ways, develop character in you. You will begin to see the big picture and continually invest into a generation that you cannot yet see with your own eyes. You will learn the principle of self-restraint and investment. You will learn how to invest your funds for long term increase and very shortly you will have funds to invest in properties, kingdom business, different assets and profitable opportunities that God will bring your way. The principles of success and prosperity will overtake you because you are becoming "Multi-Generational" in your lifestyle, focus and planning. You will fulfill the fatherhood principle of God for future generations to come, and they will be blessed because of your decisions.

See our web-site for resources and my teachings on the "multi-generational man". www.basicsforsuccess.com

Chapter 4 Review Points

- Be a multi-generational minister for God.

The Business Of Ministry

Chapter 5
Personal Help

EXTREME PERSONAL ACCOUNTABILITY

We all need to be accountable to God and to His authorities on earth. Woe to the man or woman who has no accountability or spiritual covering. I have seen many great men and women of God fall into terrible sin and disgrace because of the lack of accountability. I have also seen others walk in integrity and safety because of their extreme accountability. Accountability must be activated both vertically and horizontally if you want to be successful in ministry.

The law of sowing and reaping comes into effect with this principle. In the long term, you will reproduce who you are. The measure of your accountability to God and man will reproduce into your leaders who are under you. You cannot escape this truth. The leaders that are given under my command are my "reaping" of the accountability that I sowed in past years. If I have been unaccountable and rebellious, then I have no right to complain about my unaccountable and rebellious leaders who serve under me. Knowing this should cause us to fear God, repent and walk in extreme accountability.

The old days where a man says, *"I submit myself to God and God alone"* are over. That old story doesn't wash, and it really never has. There are no lone rangers or 007's out there that God anoints and blesses. It's just not His way, His form of government, His M.O. or His biblical standard. He anoints sons who come up under fathers. He anointed Aaron the high priest, and then the anointed garments were passed downward to his sons who were submitted to him as their father.

(Heb 13:17) Obey them that have the rule over you, and submit yourselves: for they watch for your souls, as they that must give account, that they may do it with joy, and not with grief: for that is unprofitable for you.

Who are you giving account to for your life and ministry? I recommend that you find your spiritual father, wherever he may be. *(If you don't have a spiritual father, please read the section on Spiritual Fathers)* Surround yourself with men and women of noble character and those who love Jesus more than you do (*that's a good test*). These are people that you can trust and give accountability to. Don't ever fall into giving account to a group of people who are living in sin, who don't go to church as much as you do, or who don't display the same or more fruit of the Holy Spirit as you. They will give you license to fall away and sin rather than to press towards the mark of the high calling.

I was confronting a man once about not being submitted to anyone. He told me, *"Who can I submit myself to? There is no one here on God's green earth that can handle my anointing and ministry calling. There is no one who can speak into my life that I can submit to."* That man fell into deep sin and lost his international ministry position, his wife and family, his house and fortune, and has never yet recovered after years of struggle.

I know of another man in ministry who was known world wide. He said the exact same words. Years later, he has never recovered from the train crash that crippled his once world renowned ministry.

I know another man who took a noble stand. He surrounded himself with noble men of great character, and completely submitted his life to them as well as God. He told them that he would submit his ideas, dreams, visions and revelations to them, and if they didn't agree with him, he would consider himself deceived by the enemy. This is extreme trust "personified". It's a great position of safety and strength and it requires Christ's servant hood out of everyone involved on the team. They must be walking in the Spirit of unity, faith and love in order to hear God's voice. None of them determine to hear independently from God, and they strive to keep the faith and union. This man has gone on to become one of the great men of all time in my opinion, and he has shaken nations with his ministry around the world. He's been unmovable and unshakable because he's accountable to God and to men of high caliber and honor.

Many denominational church organizations force accountability upon their pastors and leaders. They make sure that everyone is submitted and on the same page together. Sometimes this is good, but sometimes a person can feel the pressure of "law" upon them to conform rather than to give account. Some men choose this as their way of accountability, and others cannot in good conscience give account to man-based, hierarchical, corporate, governmental systems.

Many free, independent, charismatic or Pentecostal ministries don't have any accountability at all, which is *very* dangerous. These are lone rangers who ride in and out when they want to and they say and do what they want in the name of God with no accountability. This is very volatile and dangerous, and the devil can gain an easy foothold in their lives and ministries.

I recommend that you set up your ministry with a gathering of people around you that have greater integrity, character and stability than you. Make sure that they love Jesus more than you, they pray longer, they are proven and willing to lay their lives down for the Lord and to sacrifice anything for His will. If you can find these people, submit to them, give yourself to them and give full account for your actions. They are deeply in love with Jesus and you can trust their character. They'll never violate you intentionally, nor will they ever direct you in anything that will hurt you or the kingdom. You are safe in a multitude of counsel, and you can grow in peace and strength by being accountable.

Concerning ministry accountability, make sure that your books are open to the public. Give a general accounting to your church members or to whomever asks. You don't necessarily have to give a weekly accounting. I recommend that you give an annual financial statement to your church members or ministry partners. Show them what is happening with your ministry, and then make the books available to the public upon request. This adds stability and trust among your members and partners.

Our ministry is audited annually by an outside auditing firm. This keeps us accountable and gives total trust to our people. No one in our organization handles the money alone. All offerings are counted by at least two trusted deacons or elders. All deposits are cross checked. All checks and payments are double checked and audited for accuracy. Every penny goes exactly where we say it goes, and is verifiably audited. This shoots the devil and his accusers down. It will be hard for him to come in and accuse any of our people of stealing or mis-appropriating ministry funds. It frees us to operate under the safety of accountability. It also encourages others to join with us in trust because of our accountability policies.

HOW TO KNOW THE CALLING OF GOD FOR SURE

Everyone worth their salt has asked the question, *"Lord, are You calling me into Your ministry service?"* However, many don't know for sure if He is calling them and some people simply choose ministry as a career choice *(a bad move if you're not called by God).*

It's very important to know the calling of God on your life. I personally believe that the calling of God is so much larger than our nano-mindset thinking of the past which would say, *"If God is calling you, then you're a preacher who stands behind a pulpit."* It's that very mindset that has crippled the church in her ability to walk in her corporate calling.

The Business Of Ministry

(1 Cor 12:4 - 6) Now there are diversities of gifts, but the same Spirit. And there are differences of administrations, but the same Lord. And there are diversities of operations, but it is the same God which worketh all in all.

(Eph 1:18) The eyes of your understanding being enlightened; that ye may know what is the hope of his calling, and what the riches of the glory of his inheritance in the saints,

(2 Th 1:11) Wherefore also we pray always for you, that our God would count you worthy of this calling, and fulfil all the good pleasure of his goodness, and the work of faith with power:

There are diversities of callings in Christ. These callings include the call to the Kingdom of His dear Son Jesus Christ, as well as the calling to an actual inheritance that He has destined you to. There are also ministry callings of God that include five fold ministry callings, helps ministry callings, parenting, teaching and business callings.

No matter what you're called to do in this life, God wants you to know your calling and destiny personally. He wants you to give diligence to finding and fulfilling your destiny/calling. There's no reason that you have to bounce off of the walls of life like a pinball to find out where God wants you. He's made provision to know your calling and destiny.

(2 Pet 1:10) Wherefore the rather, brethren, give diligence to make your calling and election sure: for if ye do these things, ye shall never fall:

In the past, our only *"called"* people had to go to bible college and become a pastor of some kind or travel as an evangelist. But the rest of the people have suffered greatly because they have not known their callings. I firmly believe that we are all called into ministry of some kind.

- I am called by God to be a man of God and a servant of Christ and His people.
- I am called to be a husband to my wife.
- I am called to be a father to my children.
- I am called to be a friend to this world in order to win them to Christ.
- I am called to be a giver of my time, life and finances to the work of God's Kingdom, to establish His covenant.
- I am called to live in a certain location in this world at a certain time.
- I am called to serve in a local church of God's choosing.
- I am called to go into all the world, preaching the gospel to all creation, making disciples of all men and instructing them in the way commanded in the Word of God.

These are the callings of God upon my life before I am ever called into the "ministry". It's because of miscommunication in the body of Christ that much of the church lies paralyzed, sleeping and inactive. We are waiting for the "called ones" (our pastors) to do the work of God as we come to church to hear a weekly report of what they're doing and how the plan seems to be working.

The fact is that the five fold ministry gifts that are given by God are designed for the exclusive purpose of building up the body of Christ so that each member will find their calling and do the work of the ministry.

(Eph 4:11 – 13)   And he gave some, apostles; and some, prophets; and some, evangelists; and some, pastors and teachers; For the perfecting of the saints, for the work of the ministry, for the edifying of the body of Christ: Till we all come in the unity of the faith, and of the knowledge of the Son of God, unto a perfect man, unto the measure of the stature of the fullness of Christ:

70

Therefore I submit to you that every man, woman and child who is a believer in Christ is "called" into ministry. This doesn't mean that we're all speakers, orators, preachers, evangelists or that we will all stand behind the pulpit. But as members of the body of Christ, we are all called to the "Work Of The Ministry", which is so much larger than we've thought in the past. It's much more than a Sunday morning church service or Wednesday night bible study.

God called the entire nation of Old Testament Israel to be a nation of priests who would minister to a very *"lost"* world.

(Exo 19:6 KJV) And ye shall be unto me a kingdom of priests, and an holy nation. These are the words which thou shalt speak unto the children of Israel.

Today, God has issued a New Testament called for every Christian to be not only priests, but also kings because of the finished work of Jesus on the cross of Calvary. He purchased all of mankind and called us all to be priests unto God and kings upon the earth!

(Rev 1:6 KJV) And hath made us kings and priests unto God and his Father; to him be glory and dominion for ever and ever. Amen.

(Rev 5:10 KJV) And hast made us unto our God kings and priests: and we shall reign on the earth.

Are you called into the New Testament ministry? The answer to all believers is *"YES, a thousand times YES"!* Are you called to be a pastor, teacher, public speaker? Maybe, maybe not. But before we discuss the answer to this question, please let me remind you:

71

- Some are called to be the greatest mothers to their children.
- Some are called to be the greatest business men and women of all time.
- Some are called to be the greatest athletes of all time and to draw the attention of the masses for the glory of God.
- Some are called to be instructors, teachers, educators and disciplers of children, teens and young adults for the empowering of the next generation.
- Some are called to serve in government positions to truthfully represent the people of God in their designated realm of authority.
- Some are called as judges to exercise the Spirit of righteous law in the land upon the people of the land.
- Some are called to finance the message of the gospel with their unique giftings of wealth increase and business anointings.
- Some are called to possess and conquer, and to possess properties, lands, houses, buildings, cities and businesses.
- Some are called to preach the gospel, teach the Word of God build up and educate within the context of the local church.

There are many diversities of the Spirit of God and His callings, but they all work together to accomplish His will. Many people in the world today are fulfilling their callings and destinies with limited knowledge because they've never been told that this is what God has called them to do. Still many other people are totally unfulfilled in their callings because they are out of position with their true calling and purpose.

I've heard statistics indicating that 90% of America's work force must be *"watch dog"* managed in their work place. This tragic figure is because 90% of America is out of position and in the wrong place of employment. A person who is fulfilling his or her calling doesn't need to be managed or watched over because they are the perfect fit for the job and they will do it better than 1,000 others who aren't called to that job. Imagine if 90% of America was in position and not in need of management watchdog oversight to make sure that they're doing their job. What difference would that make in the productivity of corporate and business America? What difference would that make in the church? Yes, many who are working in the church are not really called to the positions that they're working in, and they're totally unfulfilled in life.

In the current American church an apostle must fill the shoes of a pastor. A prophet must also fill the shoes of a pastor. The evangelist will either struggle on the road of despair and poverty, or he will put on the shoes of a pastor in order to save his marriage, family and financial condition. The reason that these men and women are all pastors is because this is the only position that currently offers a paycheck in the old wineskin church at large. None of the other giftings are recognized by the modern day church, only the pastor.

The pastor must be a perfect businessman, administrator, preacher, teacher, evangelist, husband, parent, housekeeper, doctor of the Word of God, able to speak 6 times per week and able to clearly hear from God at any given moment, perfect at performing funerals, weddings and any other special event that comes along. He/she must be good at fund raising, finance, investing and in his/her spare time, had better be able to mow the church lawn. This old wineskin mentality has sent too many of our dearly called leaders, our brothers and sisters packing – attempting to fulfill their callings in the corporate world, serving in government family services departments, selling cars and houses or surviving elsewhere. Dearly beloved, these tragedies occur because we don't understand the callings of God.

No one should feel bad about being called into business. It's not a lower class calling! Everyone should get into position in the calling that God has for each member of the body of Christ. We'd all be fools to think that God has elected to call a few select men and women to be in His ministry, and then the rest of the masses just hang around and try to survive in this world while the ministry educates and trains them one day per week. This is crazy thinking! Every area and segment of the world must be saturated with the living, moving active Word of God in leavening action through His believers. This includes education, politics, business, service and humanitarian arenas of society. Your calling is important! It's important enough to God that He put you here to fulfill that calling.

I believe that a person can find their calling and election by God by prayer, fasting, listening, taking notes, honesty and reflection. I also believe that your calling is very closely related to your inner most desires, as God delights in giving you the desires of your heart.

(Psa 37:4 KJV) Delight thyself also in the LORD; and he shall give thee the desires of thine heart.

Methods I use to evaluate and know what a person's general callings are:

1. Write down 5 things that you absolutely love to do. You will do these things even if you have to pay to do them. These things strike passion and drive in your life and seem to fulfill you when you do them. Just talking about them puts a sparkle in your eye and a spring in your step.

1. _____

2. _____

3. _____

4. _____

5. _____

2. Next, write down 5 things that you absolutely do NOT like to do. These are things that you wish you didn't have to do, things that you try to stay away from and things that seem to steal your joy. *(for instance - book keeping or house cleaning. Some of these might actually be the things that you do every day at your job.)*

1. _____

2. _____

3. _____

4. _____

5. _____

Next, if you could only do one thing in your life for the remainder of your life, what would that one thing be? Go above to the top five things that you love to do, and choose only one of those things to be the one and only thing that you would do if forced to make that decision.

1. _____

Generally speaking, you have just brought some of your heart issues out on the table. You can now see the 5 things you love to do, the 5 things you hate to do and the one thing that you'd choose if it came to having to make an eternal life choice of one thing only. You haven't totally found your life's calling, but I can guarantee you that the five things that you love to do are a rough outline of where God is calling you. I'd call this a *"Blurry Directional Focus"* for your life. You're not seeing in total clarity, but you are beginning to see rough shapes, images and forms. Your compass is beginning to spin around to a definite focus. Your direction is looking brighter already!

We also know what you don't like to do, and what you need to stay away from. For many, this means a total change in career direction or job location. For others, this calls for getting help, education or hiring out the things that you hate to do.

I personally don't like book keeping. For years I struggled with balancing my checkbook, bouncing checks, paying my bills late and being in total disarray. This wasn't because I didn't have money, but it was because I couldn't stand the thought of sitting down and crunching numbers, writing checks, licking stamps and addressing envelopes. Book keeping could steal my joy away faster than anything! Finally, in prayer one day the Lord told me to get this area of my life in divine order. I told him that I couldn't stand doing book keeping and I was no good at it. He spoke clearly to me, *"Either go take a college class and learn it, or hire it out, but get it in order!"*. I hired a book keeper!

Years later, I've learned and schooled on how to do the books, but I still have a professional book keeper and auditor that does everything professionally. It's their calling! I laugh as we sit there with all of the paperwork and books for the year, and the auditor smiles with zeal in his eyes like a lion looking over a fresh kill! He can't wait to dig in to the auditing of the annual books. It amazes me as I tell him, *"I'm glad you're called to this and not me!"* He's fulfilling his calling, and he's getting paid well to perform this vital calling.

(Psa 37:4) Delight thyself also in the LORD; and he shall give thee the desires of thine heart.

No doubt, part of delighting yourself in the Lord is to find and chase your heart's desires. God wants to give them to you. Stop chasing the things that you feel you have to do, and start chasing your dreams, desires and things that bring you extreme joy!

PERFECTING THE FOCUS OF YOUR CALLING

Now that you have a *"Blurry Directional Focus"* of your heart's desires, begin to pray, fast, spend quality time with God, read the Word of God and search Him out with focused direction for your life. If you honestly search for Him, you will find Him. If you search His Kingdom first, He will show you the focused destiny for your life and He will open the doors for you.

(Jer 29:11 – 13) For I know the thoughts that I think toward you, saith the LORD, thoughts of peace, and not of evil, to give you an expected end. Then shall ye call upon me, and ye shall go and pray unto me, and I will hearken unto you. And ye shall seek me, and find me, when ye shall search for me with all your heart.

(Mat 6:33) But seek ye first the kingdom of God, and his righteousness; and all these things shall be added unto you.

Finally, are you called into the ministry? That's an issue of fasting and prayer. Only God can call you into His ministry no matter how bad you want to become a minister. If He doesn't call, don't waste your time trying to kick open doors that He hasn't opened. You'll end up unfulfilled and having to fabricate an anointing that's not been truly given to you by God. Your work will end in human strength, mental ascent and fabricated anointing. And if you get too much in the way of God's plan for His people, God will be forced to bring you home early in order that you don't destroy people's lives and God's divine will on the earth.

Your gift will make a way for itself. Whatever your calling, the gifting will come out of you naturally. It will bring you joy, as well as joy to those who receive the gift. Flow with your gifts and callings and fulfill them. This is God's will for you.

If you feel called into ministry, seek out a spiritual father who can train and disciple you. Begin to seek education in the field of your calling. Allow the Holy Spirit to develop your gifts and callings. I recommend that you find someone that you really admire who's operating in the gifts and callings that you feel you are called to, and follow them. Imitate them, read their books, attend their sessions, get close to them and find out what makes them do the things they do. Learn from their lives and experience. Do what Paul said to do as he instructed his followers.

(1 Cor 11:1) Be ye followers of me, even as I also am of Christ.

FINDING WISDOM WHEN YOU NEED IT

Personal humility in ministry is very important. We leaders must realize that we don't know it all, and actually we probably don't know *"at all"*. We are desperately dependant on the Holy Spirit for guidance and wisdom. In the Spirit of networking and interlinking of the body, He wants us to seek wisdom from men and women around us. Every good leader will have friends and associates surrounding him/her, who have great wisdom in given areas. The bible says that she (wisdom) is calling in the streets, looking for someone to hear her.

(Prov 1:20 – 21) Wisdom crieth without; she uttereth her voice in the streets: She crieth in the chief place of concourse, in the openings of the gates: in the city she uttereth her words . . .

Wisdom is available to anyone who will humble himself and ask. Asking is not only a good thing, it's vital if a ministry or business leader is going to survive and succeed in this earth.

(Prov 11:14) Where no counsel is, the people fall: but in the multitude of counselors there is safety.

You can never get too much counsel. The wise man will open his ears and ask. You will find that true wisdom can't wait to get to you. When you find true wisdom in a person who has the goods, you will find that it pours out of the person freely and gladly. However, it's your job to seek wisdom with all of your heart, and ask with humility, acknowledging that you are in need of answers. There is great safety in this lifestyle of humility and need for counsel. However, those who don't bother to seek for wisdom are sure to fall!

Here's a secret about in-depth wisdom. I have a friend who is the absolute best in the land at developing large mail programs for churches and large ministries. He told me an intriguing story of how he used to try to give his wisdom away. He would attempt to help his friend's ministries out by flying out to see them. He would pay for his own plane ticket, take time off from work and go to impart his wisdom into these people. Unfortunately, they'd forget to pick him up at the airport. Once he arrived at their offices, they'd want to go to lunch. They weren't really going to use his wisdom and he would go home feeling like he'd wasted their time, his time and God's time. He told me that God finally told him to charge them $5,000 per day plus expenses and stop trying to get his wisdom to them.

Phone calls began to come his way and his friends and others would ask what it would take to hear about what abilities he had. He told them $5,000 per day plus all expenses. They were astounded that he'd charge so much! Nevertheless, he began to be booked up and when he arrived at the airport, the ministry leaders were waiting for him in a limousine. When he stepped into the car, they were all in the back seats with note pads in hand, ready to get started. Lunch was 30 minutes, and they stretched the days as long as they could with him. Once he left, they actually put his wisdom to work, and in just a few months their ministries were transformed and they felt like they had spent some of the best money ever on this man's wisdom.

After he told me this story, He told me this very powerful statement. He said, *"Daniel, true wisdom is not free. As a matter of fact, wisdom costs a lot. It is impossible for me to*

The Business Of Ministry

impart true wisdom into you unless you are willing to pay for it.
It's a spiritual principle. I can't impart "deep unto deep" unless
you pay dearly for it". This powerful truth has changed my life.
Now, I don't have a problem paying thousands or hundreds of
thousands if necessary to get wisdom!

(Prov 4:7 KJV) Wisdom is the principal thing; therefore get
wisdom: and with all thy getting get understanding.

Gather men and women of wisdom around you, honor and
confide in them. Don't be afraid to make a phone call and ask
questions. Don't be afraid to ask even the hard questions that
most won't ask. And most importantly, don't be afraid to pay
for wisdom when you need to. The payment will cause you to
"inherit" that wisdom, as it becomes yours with payment.

I recommend that everyone has a spiritual father in their life.
This is one area where a true spiritual father can come in
powerfully helpful, as when a son or daughter needs true wisdom
for a problem that they're facing.

RELATIONSHIPS: WHEN TO STAY PUT
OR MAKE THE RELATIONAL CUT

I am a firm believer in covenant relationships. My desire is to be
a friend and to have friends for life. Though we may end up in
different locations, my covenant bond with friends, staff and
workers is for the rest of my life. My loyalty and faithfulness
must be forever, just like God's loyalty and faithfulness stands
firm towards me.

However there are some who will challenge your relationship,
and who will force you to make tough relational decisions that
are not easy. So, when do you stick with a relationship and
when do you cut, run and consider your losses?

80

It's not easy to shake me. Once you've got me as a friend, I don't go away easily. I can put up with a lot, and I can look past human weakness, roughness and even trouble in the relationship. However, there's one time that I will leave the relationship. That is when a person clearly begins a lifestyle of willful sin, selfish ambition or an embittered lifestyle that grows up to defile many.

I can handle it when my friend misses it. I can handle a fall, and can even handle multiple falls. However, I can't handle remaining in so-called covenant relationship when I see a so-called brother purposely violating God, His commands, His people, and His Son. Your willful rebellion and overt sin will separate me from you. Let me explain through a real life story.

I have a dear friend whom I met years ago. When I first met him, he was one of the most awesome men of God that I'd ever met. He was bold as a lion, tenacious, anointed to preach the gospel and powerful in his delivery. He was compassionate, kind hearted and made me (and everyone else around) feel like a really special person. He was a good instructor and was always offering free wisdom tips to encourage and help me along in my life and ministry. He was such a great person in my eyes that I felt like he was becoming a spiritual father to me. He was certainly a mentor at very least, and he became a good peer friend that I really looked up to. His ministry was in another country but I found opportunity to bring him into our church whenever I could and I'd travel to see him in his ministry travels in a heart beat.

However, there was a re-occurring problem that he seemed to fall victim to. This man kept having women accuse him of making sexual moves on them. I'd hear from one source that this man had been accused of making an advance on the church secretary where he was guest speaking. He'd flatly deny it and I stood with him. Then he'd been accused of sleeping with one of the worship team's wife at his church. He allegedly admitted to that and sought counsel from a friend in ministry. A year later, he was allegedly swapping wives with a head elder of his church.

81

He had been divorced a couple of times in the past for the same type of problems.

Then I found out that he had brought one of my spiritual sons and his wife into his church as a youth pastor. That concerned me greatly as I knew of this man's weakness and history. Six months later, my spiritual son was separated from his wife. I found out later that this man had been having an ongoing affair with her for almost a year while convincing her husband that he was only counseling her in her apartment night after night. Once this overt sin became public, I attempted to go to this man and find out the truth. Making a long story short, the man lied to me about the entire ordeal. He also lied to my other associates in ministry, telling us all a different story. He offered no apology or restitution to the young man who's marriage he destroyed, and that was the end of my relationship with this man.

I'm a pretty merciful man, but at that time I decided to "CUT AND RUN" from this relationship. There were many reasons that I had to do this. The credibility of my own ministry would be at stake. Aligning myself with a non-repentant man would make me guilty of the same sins. My own integrity, my spiritual and mental health, and my destiny would be forever altered if I were to align with willful sinful men. It was the hardest thing to do because I loved (and still love) this man. He's been a friend and I received much from him. However, we can never share a pulpit together and we can never minister together again. If there were a sign of repentance, maybe I'd entertain the thought of working together again a long time down the road after credibility, ethics and the fruit of repentance was evident. However, this would not take place overnight. I'm a very merciful man at heart, but mercy out of the control of the Spirit is dangerous to all involved.

Needless to say, this man has never apologized or made restitution for his actions. He's divorced and remarried for the fourth time and still pastors a church. He's lied to and deceived many in an attempt to hold on to his ministry. Rather, he should come under proper authority and receive counsel and healing. Therefore, I had to make the hard decision to "CUT AND RUN" despite my love for this man and my hope that he would repent, change and be restored.

I found out years later from another young man who was close to this fallen minister, that for a year, his new marriage relationship was on the rocks and suffering greatly under a spirit of division and divorce until he and his wife separated themselves from this man and his ministry. The day that they made the cut, their marriage problems ceased and the spirit of division left their home.

This is an extreme case. However, it should take extreme cases for us to walk away from someone and to nullify a working relationship. The spilled New Covenant blood of Jesus and our resulting relationships with family, ministry associates, friends and the people of God should mean a lot to us and we should fight for them. However, when extreme sin comes into the picture, it's time for extreme relational cuts in order to protect the mission, the team and the individual.

I've been told by the accusers that I violated covenant with this man. Actually, he violated covenant with the body of Christ when he repeatedly committed adultery with various women. He violated covenant when he violated my spiritual son's marriage *(this young man never recovered and is still out of the church to this day),* and he violated covenant when he made an open pass at my own wife.

Don't let the devil or any good intentioned Christian belittle you or heap condemnation on you for making the hard cut. Sometimes you need to "CUT AND RUN" when it's clear that the gospel of the Lord Jesus Christ is not being honored and the Spirit of God is being willfully violated. God cut himself off from Adam, and from Israel repeatedly for their willful sin and rebellion against Him. This is the Kingdom method of operation.

Your ministry, family, marriage and relationships are too valuable to allow a sinful relationship to continue or to develop in your life. God has called you to all purity and holiness, and that's hard to do when you have an offender in your midst in the name of Christian covenant relationship. Take the step and make the cut. Save yourself from a lifetime of heartache and protect the mission, the team and the individual.

Remember: Mission, Team, Individual. *(See chapter 6 on Teamwork)*

PERSONAL, BUSINESS AND MINISTRY ETIQUETTE

Business, ministry and personal etiquette is very important in this day and age of excellence. Your ministry would be well served by finding the person on your team with the highest form of etiquette and buying them some books on personal, business and ministry etiquette. Have this person send an email out to everyone once per week with an etiquette tip. Also, include your personalized comment in the email which states that this email is intended for instruction and adherence. All staff and team members are required to learn etiquette and put it into practice in the ministry.

You will find that there are certain etiquette techniques that will draw the Spirit of excellence, high quality people and finances your way. If your ministry team is willing to learn personal, business and ministry etiquette, your team will grow into God's excellence, honor and servant hood. After all, etiquette is the spirit, the attitude and the zeal with which we serve others. It seems right that we should be learning excellence in servant hood – etiquette.

Did you know that there is certain etiquette for answering the phone?

Did you know that there is a way of excellence to invite a guest speaker to your ministry?

Did you know that there is a way of excellence to honor your guests, visitors and people that you meet every day?

Did you know that etiquette will cause large doors to open wide for you in your city?

Get some etiquette books today and get started in the way of excellence, personal, business and ministry etiquette.

PROTECTION AGAINST BURN OUT

One of the sole purposes of this book is to deal with the subject of burn out. When a minister gets under too much extended pressure, dealing with too many battlefronts for an extended time, suffering from incorrect church governmental placement, walking in a ministry office that he's not called to, and lacking the grace of God to deal with continued satanic onslaught, this is a sure mixture for burn out. We are not built to endure such heavy burdens!

(Mat 11:28 - 30 KJV) Come unto me, all ye that labour and are heavy laden, and I will give you rest. Take my yoke upon you, and learn of me; for I am meek and lowly in heart: and ye shall find rest unto your souls. For my yoke is easy, and my burden is light.

I believe that this book addresses pertinent issues that will save a minister from burnout. Some of these include: God's Proper Governmental Order, The Spirit Of Honor, A Proper Covering, A Proper Way To Give & Save, Proper Financial Accountability, New & Innovative Funding Techniques, Staff Procedures, Days off & Vacations Planned, and Volunteer Help.

Burn out comes from things being out of order. Our God is one of decency and order.

(1 Cor 14:40 KJV) Let all things be done decently and in order.

It is my opinion that this book will help any minister to overcome and guard against burn out as it will help guide and lead a minister into proper governmental and administrative order.

DAILY PERSONAL EDUCATION AND BETTERMENT

It's important that you and your entire staff develop an active plan to increase your education in your fields of interest, desire and operation. Don't get so busy with the working of the ministry that you don't have time to learn and increase your education in your own field. If you fail in this area, you will wake up one day to find that an entire generation of young buccaneers has grown up around you with more success, ability and education than you have. You will find that you have nothing to give in education and teaching to the next generation of young ministers.

Remember to be multi-generational in your ministry purposes. This includes an active plan to continue your own training and education.

When you study a subject intensely for a year, you become versed in that subject. Study it for 3 years and you become very knowledgeable. Study it intensely for 5 years and you become an expert in the field. Make sure that you end up as an expert in your field by continuing your study and education. Make sure that your employees and staff are also on track towards expertise in their fields of interest, as you are building a team of experts.

Set a schedule to read 6 books on your field of interest per year. That's one every two months, which can be read after your daily prayer and devotions in the morning. Reading 3 – 4 pages of a book per day will accomplish this task.

Find trade shows, conferences, conventions and special meetings where the experts are hanging out, speaking and educating. Make sure that you attend no less than one convention or conference in your field per year.

Check up frequently with your staff to make sure that they are constantly learning and excelling in their areas of expertise. Help pay for their conferences if you can, as it will increase you by increasing them. The investment will pay for itself many times over.

Set goals to concerning your education in reference to your goals and priorities. One great way to do this is to get a hold of the "LIFE APPLICATION STUDY COURSE" which offers you the ability to track and expand the seven vital areas of your life that you must constantly educate yourself in. You can get this study course at our www.basicsforsuccess.com web site.

Chapter 5 Review Points

- Be radically accountable.
- Know the calling of God on your life.
- Develop your desires and dreams.
- Find and utilize wisdom from others.
- Develop your personal and ministry relationships based on God's Word.
- Develop and grow in etiquette.
- Guard yourself against burnout.
- Educate and better yourself daily

The Business Of Ministry

Chapter 6
Staff Help

PERSONELL PRINCIPLES, POLICIES & PROCEEDURES

POLICY MANUAL

Every ministry needs to have an active policy manual in place. This manual is the foundational working manual that dictates to whom, where, when, why and how you operate. It generally includes business, communications and phone etiquette, dress codes and guidelines of general functions and operations of the organization. It sets the needed guidelines and policies that will help direct your entire staff and volunteers in one mind, one direction, and in the excellence level that you choose to demand. Without a policy manual, you will invite upon yourself much unneeded trouble, pain and sleepless nights. The flesh of man loves a loosely run ship. The Spirit loves a tightly knit team of professionals who are willing to live within the guidelines of the policy manual for the glory of God.

While developing a policy manual, remember that you need to keep the Spirit of unity and peace. Don't develop a manual that will require stringent legalistic guidelines that will dishearten your staff. Rather, make sure that you have a staff that can easily fit within the guidelines because they are operating according to the Spirit of God's grace and excellence. Once the policy manual is set in place and is a pleasing spiritual guide for the daily operations of your ministry, the manual will uproot those who are not really with you in Spirit, in excellence and in united vision. Once these people are uprooted and exposed, you must choose to either work with them to develop their skills so

89

that they can come up to the spiritual bar quickly, or to remove them from the team for the sake of the team.

I heard Robert Kiyosaki once say in his book *'Retire Young, Retire Rich'*, *"MISSION, TEAM, INDIVIDUAL. The most important priority is the mission, then comes the team. The last in priority is the individual."* A good policy manual will help your staff focus on this very issue. People who believe the opposite – INDIVIDUAL, TEAM, MISSION must be uprooted from your staff and leadership team. They must be corrected or removed if you are to be successful in your calling and destiny.

I recommend that you go to your favorite successful ministry and humbly ask them if you could get a copy of their policy manual. You can also go to our web site at www.basicsforsuccess.com and download a free copy of a standard policy manual which you can customize to fit your needs.

Once you develop the policy manual, I recommend that you put one of your leaders in charge of the manual, to educate your staff and people, to let them know of the policies and procedures of the ministry, and to enforce the policies as needed. As the leader of your ministry, you should not have to personally police the policies unless you are just starting up and don't have a right hand person to help you. However, you should give full authority to a staff member to let them enforce the policies of your organization in the Spirit of love and excellence, for the sake of the mission and the team.

HIRE CONTRACT

Every paid staff member on your team should be under a contract for hire which states very clearly the intent, purposes, duties, requirements, etc. of that individual and/or family. Without a written contract, you are asking for much trouble in the future and your possibilities for long term employment success are low.

A contract for hire is a valuable key for both of you. First of all, it clearly communicates to your staff member exactly what you expect from him/her, as well as the guidelines, policies, duration of employment, salaries and/or benefits, and specific duties required. Your staff member needs to know exactly what you want from him. This form of communication gives clear and concise directives for a person to work within. You can include the requirements for spiritual leadership, participation requirements, daily duties, work times and so much more. Both you and your staff member will be at ease with this contract in place.

In the event that you are having troubles with an employee/staff person who can't seem to flow with your vision, work within your policies, be the spiritual leader that you need them to be, or make it to work on time, you have recourse to deal with this person according to your contract. This very spiritual document is a simple guideline of the standard of excellence that you require in return for salary and/or benefits.

An employee that is not willing to sign an employment contract is also a staff member who will not submit to your policy manual. Most likely they are also not interested in following God's contractual Word and should be avoided at all costs.

For those who think that working without a contract is more godly and spiritual, you are heading towards trouble quickly. Remember, even God was willing to write the contract that gave us our boundaries, freedoms, liberties and authority. He's willing to stick by his contract. Will you write one and stick to yours?

OBEDIENCE TO POLICIES

When you set a standard of excellence in your ministry, everyone must follow this standard from the top downward. A break in the chain of command will harm your mission and will actually instruct those beneath that chain of command that it's alright to break rank, bend rules and live apart from the policies and procedures of the ministry. You need men of Zebulun with your ministry.

*(1 Chr 12:33, 38) Of Zebulun, such as went forth to battle, expert in war, with all instruments of war, fifty thousand, **which could keep rank: they were not of double heart.***
All these men of war, that could keep rank, came with a perfect heart to Hebron, to make David king over all Israel: and all the rest also of Israel were of one heart to make David king.

Don't allow breaking of rank or double mindedness. Be quick to deal with any policy breaking spirit on your team.

PLANNED TRAINING SESSIONS

It's vital to care for your leadership team. Instruction, education and training are very important. One of the most important things that you can do to train your team is to be with them. We find that Jesus was always with his 12 followers. He instructed them, shared His life with them and spent quality time with them. Make sure that your time with your staff is quality in nature, on purpose and with a passion for what you are all called to do.

Set a time for your staff to meet at least once per month, preferably in the evening. Make the setting as casual as possible, at your home or in a "non business" location. Plan to spend a designated time of one hour (no more) instructing your staff in deep principles of the Word of God, allowing them to see your true passion, heart and vision. Make the time special to them. Close the meeting and make it "by invitation only". I have taken

12 monthly sessions with my leaders and delivered my 12 top priorities for Christian life into their hearts. I thought to myself, If I had 12 hours to live and had to impart the most important aspects of life, ministry, vision and focus to a group of select faithful men and women, what would those subjects be? This 12 session series as well as other helpful resources are available at www.basicsforsuccess.com .

Impart your heart to your staff and key leaders during this time. Start off with some snacks, fun and laughter, fellowship and communication. Then deliver your message to them in less than one hour. Give a little time for discussion and cross pollination of ideas and thoughts, then close the meeting with a short prayer and end in fellowship. This will be some of the most productive time you can ever have with your staff members.

DELEGATION – LET GO!

One lesson that I must constantly re-teach myself is the lesson of delegation. A great leader has the ability to pick out and train up a faithful leader, and then to delegate authority and responsibility to that person. A great leader can even allow that person to fail and still help them to learn from the failure and come back stronger than ever.

Many of us stop the size and growth of our ministries because of our lack of ability or unwillingness to delegate. If you want to grow and increase, you must delegate!

Delegation is the giving of both responsibility and authority. Don't ever give one without the other. American school teachers are given the responsibility to educate our children without the authority to enforce the educational process. As a result, they have a hard time doing their jobs and many students don't really get trained, but are passed along through the system to graduate without meeting the adequate requirements.

In the same way, a ministry staff member who has a great responsibility given to him or her will grow tired and weary and may even quit or cause trouble if authority is not also given to that person to complete the task. Imagine a person who's given the job to pay the bills, but is given no money to pay them. Imagine a person who must walk in the responsibility to instruct a bible college class, but has no authority to demand that classroom disciplines are followed and that students turn in their papers on time. Imagine a church secretary who is given the responsibility to direct the daily operations of the church office, but who's been given no authority to make a decision or to send callers to the proper channels. She doesn't even have a key to open up the church office. This lack of delegating of authority with responsibility will be disastrous!

Leader, you've got to let go of the personal responsibilities that are tying down your very busy day and delegate them to faithful men who can handle these areas for you.

(2 Tim 2:2) . . . the same commit thou to faithful men, who shall be able to teach others also.

Give out the responsibility and the authority to complete the task. Check up on the individual and ask them to give you a periodic update as to the program that they've taken over. Help them to make important decisions if they need the help, but let them run and learn. If they fall, meet with them and teach them how to not make the same mistake again. They must realize that they're standing in your shoes and making decisions for you, therefore it's important to make the decisions that you'd make and try to do it the way you would do it within reason. Their success is critical for your success and the success of the mission and the team. However, a mistake is not the end of the delegation process. It's an opportunity to disciple your staff member and to help them turn the mistake into success.

As long as failure is not deemed as a terrible occurrence in a person's life and ministry (and it's not), people won't be terrified of failure and reprisal for making an honest mistake. It's important that you help your staff to learn through failure and use those times as an instructional time of building up and strengthening.

One of my spiritual fathers says, *"My ministry used to be like the inside of a clock. I'd be the little wheel spinning around and around just to get the big wheels to move a little bit. I wore myself out doing that. Then I figured out delegation and now I'm the big wheel. When I turn just a little bit, it sends the entire clock (organization) into fast movement. The slightest move on my part turns my entire organization, and the little wheels are now the ones buzzing around."*

Preventing Burnout Tip:
Remember, you must become the big wheel in your ministry that turns just a little, and the entire organization moves and spins quickly. This is only done through delegation. If you feel like the little wheel that's doing all the spinning, it's time to repent and delegate to faithful men.

TEAMWORK

It's clear that big things are done through teams, and small things are done by individuals. If your ministry can be accomplished by you alone, your vision is an individual vision of small proportion which can be handled by your own abilities. However, if you're going to do anything great for the Kingdom of God, you will need to develop a great team of faithful people around you, and you will have to be a great leader among them all to pull them together into one vision and focus.

How many people does it take to run a small solo music ministry? Usually one – the singer. How many people does it take to run a large solo music ministry? An entire team of professionals, engineers, technicians, audio and lighting professionals, concert managers, venue managers, product managers, designers, volunteer coordinators, promoters, executives, artists, musicians, singers, distribution companies and retail store outlets just to start. Do you see the difference in large vision vs. small vision? Teamwork is vital for a large vision. If your vision is too large for you to do it on your own, then you must rely on teamwork. Become the leader necessary to develop a team around you that can bring the vision into reality. Study leadership skills that you need to pull together and keep a team together. Find others who are currently succeeding in what you want to do and learn from them. Get wisdom and develop your team-building skills. Wisdom is always found in a multitude of counselors.

Prov 11:14 Where no counsel is, the people fall: but in the multitude of counselors there is safety.

DIVISION, COMPETITION & FAVORITISM

A good discipleship ministry will encounter competition and fear of favoritism from time to time among those being discipled. This is as normal as when it happens among your own children. However, you can stop this divisive spirit from gaining a foothold in your ministry by constantly confirming your staff and leaders among one another and among your people. It's important that you build your staff up and tell them the qualities that you see in them, in full view of every one of them. This open and honest acceptance of them all will promote unity and respect among them, and will keep the fear of favoritism far from your ministry.

Good fathering and mothering skills are required when there is favoritism portrayed among the leaders and staff. It's important to be sensitive to your entire staff, and realize their needs and acceptance levels. One staff member will be a real work horse and never need encouragement and public recognition because he is secure in the calling of God on his life. However, there might be one who needs additional and extra recognition due to fear, weakness or past life traumas. Instead of fighting this, understand what your staff needs and help them through it. Additional encouragement of the weaker vessel in front of the others will train them all how to be sensitive to the needs of the weaker ones on the team, and will give them the training they need to handle the same situation in their future.

I'm not saying that you should cater to a great deficit in people's lives. Hopefully you wouldn't have brought someone on board as a staff/leadership position with such a deficit. However, I'm talking about natural weakness among "sons" in the ministry, those that you're actively discipling and who are under your spiritual parental authority to build up, encourage, instruct and train.

TEAM INHERITANCE

It's important for staff to know that they're working with the team, laying their lives down and giving their best for a great mission. In that mission, there needs to legitimately be something there for the team members called an inheritance. Everyone needs to know that they're building a Kingdom that they're part of. They'll give their all for it if they know that they're going to inherit it.

I'm not talking about giving the pulpit ministry over to the secretary as her inheritance. I'm not saying that you have to give the ministry over to your elders in 10 years for their faithful service. However, there are some deeper areas of inheritance that many people are looking for, especially *"sons"* in the ministry who want to dedicate their lives to your vision and ministry.

True sons are looking for a true father who will always be with them, always help them, always encourage them and who will never leave them or forsake them. This is an inheritance that you can offer your staff and leaders.

True sons are looking for a double portion of your anointing. They want to be instructed, trained, corrected and sent out into the world. They need to be patted on the back and encouraged to go out and do double of what you were able to do during your ministry lifetime. This is an inheritance that you can offer your staff and leaders.

True sons are looking for covenant relationship and a helping hand, someone who loves them like a father and who will correct them when they need it. They want to know that you are with them for the rest of their lives as an encourager, instructor, friend and helper. They need to know that you will stand with them if they fail or fall. They want to know that it's OK with you if they're not perfect, and that you're that one person that they can call upon any time they need help. This is an inheritance that you can offer your staff and leaders now and forever.

This is the inheritance of family, fatherhood and son-ship. It's the basis of Christ's relationship with His Father, and the relationship that we've been invited into with the Father through Jesus Christ. It's the example that Jesus left with His disciples as well.

It's important to offer long lasting family relationship as a part of the inheritance of your ministry. I also recommend that you remind your staff and leaders that the ministry is their ministry. In other words, if not for your praise and worship leader, there would be no worship ministry. This is their ministry, accomplished by them for the people. They own this ministry and the credit for the anointing upon that ministry goes to them to the glory of God. They have the great responsibility of filling large shoes when it comes to worship ministry, and if they fulfill the duty well, they need to be honored for it and recognized as the owner of this anointing. It's their inheritance.

What a privilege it is to have staff and leaders who offer their gifts and callings to build your vision! Give them the inheritance that's due to them while they selflessly serve your vision with all their hearts. With the confidence of knowing that you're with them as a father whether they're up or down, strong or weak, in good times and bad, they will give their lives for you to the very end!

SIN AND ATTITUDE PROBLEMS

There are some problems that must be dealt with quickly and with precision. Among them are willful sin, rebellion and attitude problems. There can be no delay when these problems arise in your ministry. Waiting too long to deal with these areas can be deadly to your ministry or set you back months or years in your progression and team spirit.

WILLFUL SIN

Sin is termed many times in the bible as "mark missing". Missing the mark of the high calling on purpose is a lifestyle that cannot be tolerated on a leadership team. When a person has decided to walk in sin as a lifestyle, his or her leadership capabilities are over. They won't be restored until he or she gets help, healing, restoration and a restored passion for living a holy life free from sin. Don't make the fatal mistake of sweeping willful sin under the carpet and hoping that it will go away. It will grow into a monster that will consume the forward

99

progression of your ministry, and it will eat much of your seed that has been sown in faith as a ministry. Don't cut your harvest short by allowing monsters to eat your seed.

REBELLION

Any act of rebellion against authority must be dealt with quickly and with skill. No rebellion can ever be permitted on a leadership team. Leaders must know and understand this, and must be immediately corrected if they ever fall into rebellion. Depending on the style of leadership you walk in, you will either be a person of a second chance, or you will be a "one strike and you're out" person. Your decisions in whether to offer a second chance or not will be according to the grace that God has given you.

ATTITUDE PROBLEMS

When attitudes become a problem, the Spirit of God is not leading the person(s) with the problem. There is no attitude problem with anyone who walks in the Spirit.

(Gal 5:22 – 26) But the fruit of the Spirit is love, joy, peace, longsuffering, gentleness, goodness, faith, Meekness, temperance: against such there is no law. And they that are Christ's have crucified the flesh with the affections and lusts. If we live in the Spirit, let us also walk in the Spirit. Let us not be desirous of vain glory, provoking one another, envying one another.

The Spirit of God never has an attitude problem. It's only the flesh of man who has attitude problems. Realize the spirit that you're dealing with. Never allow attitude problems to gain access into your ministry team, but rather instruct your team to keep their attitudes crucified with Christ. If the problem persists, deal with the person(s) in private first, in public secondly and then dismiss them from the team if they are unable to walk in the Spirit.

FIRING STAFF AND LEADERS

One of the worst nightmares for many leaders is the thought of having to fire a team member, staff or leader. However, this task requires great leadership skill. When it's time to fire a person, you must remember the following principle:

MISSION - First
TEAM - Second
INDIVIDUAL - Last

The mission is at stake, the one that God has called you to lay your life on the line for. The team is also counting on your leadership to keep the unity, spiritual health and forward progression of the team together so that you can fulfill the mission. The individual comes last in the above scenario.

Your desire to ostrich-hole the problem in hopes that it will go away must not stop you from taking action that you know you must take. Remember, your personal feelings are individual ones which must take a back seat to the mission and team.

Your hope that the individual could somehow change, transform, be rehabilitated, etc. is an individual hope. If you're being led by this hope, you're looking out for the individual rather than for the mission or the team. You must die to the desire to not act, for the sake of the mission and the team.

Firing a person for the sake of the mission and the team shows the highest form of love for the one being fired *(the individual)*, the team and the mission *(God)*. You must relieve the person of the duty that they're failing in so that they can re-direct their focus or receive the healing/ministry he/she needs to be a success in another field and on another team. As a leader, it's your responsibility to make the critical decision to fire and replace team members when it's clearly time.

This doesn't mean that you can't still be a friend, a father and mentor to the individual. If he will allow, you can still stand with the individual as he finds his new place in life and accept the correction and change necessary to make him productive on another new team of God's choosing.

FUN – CREATE IT

Ministry is hard work and many times it can be overwhelming! Leading a ministry with people and their problems is dirty work and requires the power of God to keep you strong and vigilant. There have been times in my ministry that I thought I was going crazy as I was dealing with unrepentant homosexuals, sexually pro-active people who were trying to entice our church members, youth struggling with drug addictions, a person in trouble with the legal system, two potential bankruptcies in the church and an angry mother who didn't like what the youth pastor said during last week's youth message. I know a pastor of a large church (3,000 +) who says that a day doesn't pass in their office where an absolute tragedy doesn't come into their office – a death, robbery, divorce, murder, lawsuits and the like.

If you don't MAKE your ministry fun and exciting, you will quite possibly go crazy or get embittered and lose your ministry destiny. Ministry is the highest calling on the planet and is also one of the hardest. It's taxing on a human being to be caring for other's needs, sin, trouble and tragedy. It can be exhausting to say the least. However, you can make ministry fun and exciting! Develop a reward system and a built-in program of fun that will take the weight and pressure of ministry off of you and your direct staff. *(also see the burnout section in chapter 5 "Protection Against Burnout").*

Find out what you and your staff like to do for fun and excitement. Do you like fellowship and movies? Play golf? Fishing? Shopping? Set times for you and your staff to go do these things. Make actual plans on the calendar to take that short trip, go fishing or golfing for a day, or to take a shopping trip somewhere special. These are planned events that you and the staff will look forward to. They're ministry sponsored events and everyone on staff is asked to go. During this time, the office closes and the cell phones are turned off *(if possible).*

You will find that these little activities will be the highlights of your week, and the staff will begin to look forward to the next planned event that you have. Set these events at a pace that you're comfortable with. God will provide for you to do this, as an uplifted staff will be a more productive and strengthened staff. Set the next "fun" event on the calendar and make sure that the staff knows about it well in advance. Watch how they start getting creative and begin dreaming about this event. This little perk will cause ministry staff to be willing to press through just about anything.

(Heb 12:2) . . . who for the joy that was set before him endured the cross, despising the shame, and is set down at the right hand of the throne of God.

Other types of fun are needed in the ministry. Church services should be fun. Children's ministry and youth group should be fun. Missions trips should be extremely fun. If people can't have fun doing something for the Lord, then they're probably not in the right position or program. **God's will is closely related to a person's desires and dreams.** He wants to give us the desires of our hearts. When this happens, this is the ultimate of "FUN".

Are you and your ministry staff having fun while you do what you do? If not, you might want to consider cutting the program or finding a creative way to fulfill your heart's desires while working through that particular part of the ministry.

DAY OFF – MAKE IT!

(Gen 2:2 - 3) And on the seventh day God ended his work which he had made; and he rested on the seventh day from all his work which he had made. And God blessed the seventh day, and sanctified it: because that in it he had rested from all his work which God created and made.

God took one day off after working six. This was called His day of rest and he blessed that day and sanctified it. Later in the old testament he commanded His people Israel to take that seventh day off to rest from their work. He was clear in his command to these people.

There is a rejuvenating blessing that comes from God when His men and women take a day off from work to rest, relax and enjoy life apart from the daily work load. Ministers especially need time off from their ministry position to keep their mind cleared, to stay focused and to keep from burning out or becoming weary in well doing.

God has commanded that you take a day off. The only other way is for you to sin *(miss the mark of His high calling)* by working seven days per week. Those who do this are normally a day late and a dollar short. However those who submit to this command are always in greater physical, mental and spiritual shape, and God gives them more money than if they were to work that extra day.

I remember when I was seventeen and I worked for a construction crew through Summer. We worked seven days per week while building an important highway. I arrived on the job at 7 AM and I left at 8 PM every day for three months. I became so disoriented and confused that I didn't know which day it was, which week it was or which month it was. I lost a lot of senses and understanding of times and seasons, and my brain literally began to shut down on me in many areas. Though I was making good extra overtime cash, my body and soul were suffering greatly for it. I lost my purpose, drive and focus to a never-ending job that devoured three months of my life. Thank God that job came to an end and I regained my senses.

Don't become one of the new super hero ministers who can defy all boundaries and set new standards in Jesus' name. Don't buy the lie that you can work seven days per week without consequence. You will pay the piper for your disobedience through lost vision, direction, focus and lack of rejuvenating time with your family, friends and God.

A day off – make it.

VACATION – TAKE IT!

A ministry leader needs serious vacation time! Re-focusing, re-fueling, getting away from the natural elements of your home town and people's problems, and getting away from spiritual oppressions of your area are vital to the health of a minister. You spend your entire life building other's lives and dealing with faults, weaknesses and sin. Many of the sins that you encounter and must help people out of are horrible and almost unthinkable. You must get freedom and relief from this once in awhile. Your spirit, soul and body need a good cleansing from the daily activities of the ministry trenches. Every minister needs a cleansing time away from constant exposure to the *"unthinkable sins"* of mankind.

I personally recommend 4 weeks per year of vacation for an active minister who is involved in working with a lot of people. Why so much vacation time? Let me tell you why.

The Business Of Ministry

When I was single and growing as a youth minister, my church gave me a couple weeks of vacation time per year. I never took it. There was no time for vacation, because the needs were so great. I knew that I'd take the vacation time at a later time once the ministry was in greater order and could afford my absence. Besides, I was broke and my measly youth ministry salary barely paid the monthly bills. I worked continually week after week, month after month, year after year. Things never improved. The ministry could never afford my absence because there were always problems that needed me. I was also developing a terrible habit of *"NOT"* taking vacations.

People would invite me to come along on vacations. I declined. I was singly focused and the ministry needed me. I watched my pastor go on vacation and I lent him my fishing pole while he was gone. I wouldn't be needing it. I was too busy with the ministry. He'd always come home with great pictures of fish caught in a beautiful river or lake.

It didn't take too long for me to realize that I had developed a lifestyle that was not beneficial to my spiritual, mental or physical health. I found that I couldn't take a vacation even if I wanted one. I began to feel burned out. When little troubles came in the youth ministry, I blew them out of proportion and they looked bigger to me than they should have. I had locked myself into a single focus of ministry, and had left the rest of my life out of the picture. Thank God I wasn't married with children, as that would have been a perfect lifestyle for a divorce and some embittered children.

Just the same as taking a mandatory day off per week, a minister needs vacation time to get away and recuperate from the constant drain of ministry. A vacation is like a fuel tank fill up or a new battery in your car. It's refreshing and energizing to say the least. It allows you to spend time with family and friends, and it allows you to see some of the world that God wants you to behold.

Again, I recommend that a minister takes 4 weeks of vacation per year if at all possible. Any church that really loves their pastor or active church leaders will force them to take multiple weeks of vacation per year. If my pastor is worn out, I'm personally in trouble. If my ministry leader is suffering from burn out or from too much output and not enough input, then I and my family are in deep trouble. Ministry leaders must take some sort of vacation to get away.

If you are a minister with a wife and children, I recommend the following vacations:
1. One vacation out of town with your wife and children to build your family.
2. One vacation in town with no church contact to fix and repair the home, take care of local needs and see some of your local city.
3. One vacation exclusively with your wife to build the most important relationship that you have – your marriage.
4. One ministry conference that you, your wife and children can go to for spiritual impartation.

You will find that these vacations are well worth the money spent, and they will keep you supercharged and ready for any battle or any problem that you must confront.

I believe that it's important that you preach to your congregation, staff and leaders on the importance for personal vacation time for any Christian. As silly as it seems, many church people can be selfish, resentful and bothered when they hear that their pastor is away on another vacation instead of in the pulpit every Sunday. However if you instill the principle deeply into their lives and encourage them to practice the vacation principle, they will receive personal benefit from their own vacation. Then they will be excited to see you taking a week to get energized for the benefit of the ministry. They'll be more willing to let you go without selfish feelings because they'll know that they will benefit from a refreshed ministry leader.

PRAYER
A MUST FOR ALL STAFF MEMBERS

Prayer is vital for any ministry team. I've always believed these coined sayings:

"The ministry that prays together stays together."

"When it comes to this ministry vision, if you can't pray, you can't play."

"You will only go as far as your prayer life, absolutely no further."

Prayer does many things for a ministry team. It unites the team in one accord, it reveals the hearts of the team members, it focuses the team vision and direction on God's intention, and most importantly, it brings corporate communication to God who loves to answer fervent, effectual, corporate prayer.

Team unity is vital to any ministry in this day and age. Without corporate unity, your ministry will not prosper to it's fullest intent.

(1 Cor 1:10) Now I beseech you, brethren, by the name of our Lord Jesus Christ, that ye all speak the same thing, and that there be no divisions among you; but that ye be perfectly joined together in the same mind and in the same judgment.

(Eph 4:3) Endeavoring to keep the unity of the Spirit in the bond of peace.

Ministries need to have set times of prayer together. Besides a true commitment to personal prayer and fasting, the team should come together "on purpose" to pray for the vision, direction, the people involved in the ministry, your community, city, nation, leaders, etc. It's also important that someone on the ministry team bring a brief teaching on prayer before each prayer session, so that people are educated and learn through the prayer experience.

Encourage fervent and tenacious prayer. Teach your leaders how to search the scriptures and then pray the scriptures in reference to your ministry calling and vision. Encourage every leader to pray out loud, to take turns and be heard individually. This is important as prayer reveals the heart of a man, and it's important that everyone on the team hears one another's heart. This in itself can calm a thousand storms! When you know someone's heart, you can see past their weaknesses. When you don't know a person's heart, it's clear that you haven't prayed much with that person.

I personally recommend that your ministry develop a solid time of prayer with leadership, and a time of prayer involved with the people and volunteers in your ministry. Prayer will dictate the power and position of your ministry in your community.

(Mat 26:40) And he cometh unto the disciples, and findeth them asleep, and saith unto Peter, What, could ye not watch with me one hour?
Mat 26:41 Watch and pray, that ye enter not into temptation: the spirit indeed is willing, but the flesh is weak.

Always remember that Satan desires to stop the prayers of the church. Any time you find that you're starting to schedule out prayer, cut down the prayer time or stopping prayer services in order to comfort the people, realize that you are being tempted by your adversary to cut your spiritual supply and power lines of communication and effectiveness. Don't allow prayer cut backs!

(Heb 10:25) Not forsaking the assembling of ourselves together, as the manner of some is; but exhorting one another: and so much the more, as ye see the day approaching.

109

(Eph 6:18) Praying always with all prayer and supplication in the Spirit, and watching thereunto with all perseverance and supplication for all saints;

(Phil 4:6) Be careful for nothing; but in every thing by prayer and supplication with thanksgiving let your requests be made known unto God.

Comfort cuts are very dangerous for any ministry. Remember that the Spirit will comfort you through prayer and fasting. The life of a Christian must be seasoned with a refusal of comfort when it comes to fasting and prayer. The Spirit will comfort you as you pray. However, Spirit comfort and flesh comfort are clearly two different things.

Prayer cutbacks are simply acts of the flesh, and are satanically induced to rob any ministry of it's true power and destiny. Therefore, make it a policy to meet with your leaders and pray!

Chapter 6 Review Points

- Have an active policy manual in place.
- All paid staff members should be under contract.
- Require obedience to policies.
- Train your leaders.
- Be willing to delegate.
- Let your ministry vision be big.
- Give your team an inheritance.
- Deal with sin and attitudes swiftly.
- Create fun for staff members.
- Take vacations and days off.
- Encourage tenacious prayer.

Chapter 7
Ministry Help

MINISTRY ADVERTISING

In this day and age there are a few things that every ministry and church must have in place if you are going to communicate effectively with your people. These items include business cards for all leaders, a nice sign in the front of your building, and signage and creative pictorials of what your ministry is doing in the community and world which people can see when they come into your church.

Your ministry needs a nice informative web site which is built to current standards. Don't buy a $50 program and try to build it yourself if you are trying to portray excellence. Let a professional do your site for you. Find a college student or a person who's willing to do it cheap rather than spend thousands of dollars to have a boutique internet design company take your church funds (*my personal opinion*).

You must begin to collect and utilize email as a realistic source of communication. People are signing on to the internet at astronomical rates and this is the best free advertising that you could possibly offer. A personal email to a church member, visitor or prospective visitor is the best way to reach today's "Sight & Sound" generation.

Make sure that your telephone system is up to date. You must be able to take the call or have a message system receive your messages for you, and have those messages forwarded to whoever should take the call. Fast call returns are vital to cutting edge ministry today. Don't run from calls, run to them. God will have many people call you if you are willing to greet the phone call with excitement and perceived opportunity for ministry.

BURNOUT PREVENTION TIP:
If you find yourself running from the phone or find that you allow it to ring too many times before you answer, and if your attitude is not excited about who may be on the other end of the phone, then you are undoubtedly involved in a project or ministry that you shouldn't be in. You need to delegate the phone call to a staff member or volunteer (see delegation chapter) or drop the program immediately.

Make sure that your phone receptionist is excited and thrilled to answer the ministry phone. People can tell when you're honestly interested in their needs. People can also tell when someone is *"bothered"* by their call.

Find every free resource in your city or area that you can utilize for advertising. Many newspapers will list your church free of charge. Christian phone directories, publications, newsletters, e-newsletters and local web sites will frequently give free listings to churches and ministries. Utilize this free gift. Pay for other advertising that's going to get you out into the public eye so God has a banner, a sign, an advertisement, etc. to draw people to. It's hard for God to draw people to a church that only exists in their own little building. Get out in the public eye so people will be drawn to your ministry. This is called advertising.

Every ministry needs a brochure which explains who you are and what you do in your community. Make this available to every visitor and wherever you can give this information to your community.

Develop a great visitor's packet as well, with all information that a person would need to find out about your ministry and your programs available. Some ministries offer a personal greeting cassette or CD in the packet which is a great addition.

Your church bulletin can be a real source of promotion for your church, or it can be a traditional waste of time. Find some of the greatest bulletins of all time by going to ministries of excellence that you look up to. Gain wisdom and learn what they're doing with their cutting edge bulletin. Implement news, reviews, events, community interaction, advertising of all sorts, pictures, awards, honors, etc. Turn your bulletin into a mini newspaper that promotes all of your areas of ministry. The one time that you have everyone in the house together should be productive and informative for all.

In the day and age of big screen projectors, multi media and computers, you can now present your programs, events, pictures, advertisements, special announcements, etc. through presentation software or video. This is a great way to inform people of what's coming up before and after a church service or meeting event.

Television is a great tool to get the word out about your church. These days, a church can get started with a nice local cable TV program for a small equipment investment of $15,000 or less including a nice computer and some digital cameras and a microphone. Most cable television stations have a local access or public access channel that you have local right to get on. Work with the cable company and try to meet their demands with equipment and the tape format that they request. If they give you a hassle and tell you that there's no place for your show, they're most likely lying to you. They feel that you are another one of the 500 churches who's called and asked what it would take to get on the air, and that you're not going to follow through any way. So they make it easy for you by saying there's no air time.

If your cable company has a *PUBLIC ACCESS* channel, that's exactly what that channel is for...public access. You theoretically could take a VHS video tape in there and they would have to play it, as long as there's no nudity, obscenity or commercial value to the program. However, your church service is a great community program that can go on public access and you have been given the right to air your program according to FCC rules, regulations and federal law.

If your cable company has a *LOCAL ACCESS* channel and they most likely do, then you can put your television show on the air for a small portion of the normal fees that a cable company charges on other stations. This fee is governed by the FCC according to the number of stations the cable company has, and how much revenue the cable company is bringing in through those stations. The fee is minimized so that local businesses and organizations can afford to have their views, opinions and programs shown to the community.

I helped a friend in Missouri to set his church up with a television program for just a few thousand dollars, and we then proceeded to negotiate with the local cable company to give him some time on the local access channel. We ended up getting him air-time for $6 per hour. I called and asked him if he wanted one show per week or 20 shows per week. At that rate, he could almost afford to be on all day long! Since that time, his TV ministry has grown to other cable and broadcast stations in the area as well. He is now ministering to more people in his area than any other ministry because of that little start-up program. God has blessed him indeed!

If you are seriously interested in television ministry, here's a simple list of video equipment that will get you started.

- 2 or 3 digital cameras and tripods
- Digital video/audio mixer
- Non-linear digital video computer

- Wireless lapel and/or handheld microphone
- Transmitting headsets for camera personnel to communicate with
- Video tape recorder unit to output your final shows onto
- Professional lighting for the area to be video taped
- Cabling and wires
- *(contact a video professional to learn more)*

Radio is another great way to put the word out. If you can get some time on a Christian radio station and feel that you have a continual message to deliver, it's a good investment to reach the Christian community and to find searching Christians. However, if you want to reach the lost you need to get airtime on a secular radio station in your area. Get creative and meet a community need through your program or advertisement and maybe the station will actually let you on the air. However, if you want to do the old school church thing with no creative flare whatsoever, you're asking the wrong people. The world's radio stations are very creative and cutting edge. They're not interested in old school radio shows for the most part.

Our web-site offers links to further resources and consortium group companies who can help you with your television/radio needs. They would be glad to help you get started and to help polish up your programming ideas. www.basicsforsuccess.com .

There are many other forms of advertising, but the key is to do whatever it takes, get to where the people are, deliver your message and ministry information to them, and be the salt of the earth that God has called you to be.

SECRET HIDDEN RESOURCE
"VOLUNTEERS"

The single largest hidden resource that a ministry can have is it's volunteer base of people. Man hours put together for projects are worth huge dollar amounts. No company can afford to do what a volunteer base of people can do. A company that has to pay it's employees an hourly wage can never compete with an activated volunteer church base. Imagine what you can do with 20 people and an 8 hour Saturday. That's 160 man hours, worth at least $1,600 in salary. Translate that into a fund raiser or an outreach program, and you will get a lot of bang for your volunteer dollar!

Any successful ministry has mastered the art of maintaining volunteers. These volunteers do FREE what any other organization has to pay for. They build buildings, mow lawns, do specialty work, maintain schools and training classes, educate, train and instruct.. They represent the church on missions trips that they personally raise the funds for. They reach out in evangelism, cleanup outreaches and door to door greetings. They fix meals, give away food, care for children and drive the youth to their next group destination. They run audio/video equipment and television cameras. They scrub toilets, sweep the floors and shampoo the carpets, serve the food, count the money, attend to the people's needs, usher during services, and so much more. Indeed, a church could never function if it had to pay for each of these services rendered. Also, a church that lacks in volunteers probably has membership problems in the areas of critical judgment, self centeredness, and generally unhappy members. Volunteers equal giving. Givers are for the most part, happy people. Non-givers are generally critical, unhappy and sour.

Volunteers need various things to keep them healthy. Some require personal attention. Some require public recognition as their catalyst for giving. Some need an occasional encouraging word from the pastor. Others just appreciate a free slab of pizza.

Regardless of which category your volunteers fall into, they all want to know that their services are appreciated, valued and that they've done something eternal for the Kingdom of God.

God promises that whatever a man sows, that will he also reap *(Gal. 6:7)*. It's important to deliver these biblical truths to your volunteers, reminding them that God will repay them for their giving. It's also important to constantly remind volunteers of the eternal work that is being accomplished, and let them know when someone's life is changed because of their giving. This is vital to the continued health of a volunteer.

We have a program that requires around 20 volunteers to work 5 hours, one Saturday morning per month. We deliver emergency food boxes to the needy and sometimes have two semi-truckloads of food to deliver. At 5:30 am, we have an assembly line of people who each put a couple of items into the boxes as they come through. We then put the boxes into the trunks of cars that drive through to receive their food box. The work is hard and it's outside, meaning that it could be freezing or hot depending on the season. However, our volunteers don't want to stop doing this program. They see themselves on a video at church the Sunday afterwards, receive a thank you from the pastor from the pulpit, and they see lives changed each time they do this. They're thrilled at helping their community, and they see continual fruit! They're also reminded that God is caring for them because they care for the poor

Prov 19:17 He that hath pity upon the poor lendeth unto the LORD; and that which he hath given will he pay him again.

Teen volunteers can be some of the best in the world. They have time and they're looking for adventure. They don't have jobs or big bills to pay and they're basically free to serve and help out. If you can tap into the hidden resource of teen volunteers, you will have gained much strength in your ministry.

117

I have found that it's important to make a win/win trade with teen volunteers for the most part. They are willing to give, but it helps when they're going to get something in return. It's important to interweave something very fun along with what you need to be done. You can offer the fun activity in exchange for the volunteer time spent. Many teens who are limited with their funds will gladly work for the church program if it means getting to do something fun and exciting afterwards.

Our teens are great volunteer fund raisers. They are almost experts in the field, and every year they pay for a multi-thousand dollar *"Summer Discipleship Training Camp"* through simple fund-raising. They raise the funds and they hit their goals. Why? If they hit their fund-raising goals, there's a free all-you-can-eat pizza party in store for them as a reward. As we have learned, teens will do anything for a pat on the back and a slab of pizza! We've also taken them to the driving range, goofy golf, shopping malls, short trips, go-cart tracks, etc. for reaching volunteer goals. These volunteers are ours for life (at least through their teen years) because we make volunteering fun, rewarding and full of fellowship.

For more resources on fund raising for your ministry, go to our website at www.basicsforsuccess.com . A good fund raising book will help you to raise thousands of dollars with your volunteer base instead of hundreds. It will permanently transition you from bake sales and car washes to new and innovative 21st century fund raising techniques that bring a much larger reward.

HANDLING SENSITIVE INFORMATION AND PASTORAL CONFIDENCE

Any time you're in ministry you will deal with very sensitive information and confidentialities the way that you deal with this

118

information can be critical to the existence of your ministry and even your natural health.

God's servants must be willing and able to handle sensitive information with extreme confidence. This means that once you find out about gross sin in a counseling situation, you can't take this information outside of the realm of authority for your own purposes. This information is not available for dinner table discussion. It should never be heard by your children, and it should never be discussed with anyone who doesn't have direct authority to answer the problem. Revealing sensitive and confidential information is not only unethical from a biblical priesthood perspective, but it's diametrically opposed to God's covering mercy that gives grace to a person and covers them while they're dealing with sin and error. Many people have lost the confidence of their people, their church members and their community by revealing confidential matters. *Just as an attorney, doctor or psychiatrist is bound to confidentiality, so also are God's ministers bound to confidentiality according to New Testament government.* There is a process for dealing with sin, and that process starts with extreme confidentiality and covering of the person in sin while they work through the repentance, restoration and needed restitution from that sin.

It's important that you have your policy manual set with clear definitions for counseling and handling of sensitive materials.

Prayer requests written on offering envelopes are just as confidential as a confessed sin in the counseling room. Financial statements, credit card numbers, bank account information, a person's signature, counseling notes and the like are all considered highly sensitive information and cannot be seen by just anyone in your organization.

Ministry policy must include the understanding that what is seen in the office stays in the office. What is heard in the office stays in the office. Even spouses of staff and leaders don't need to know what's going on in the office of counsel. They have no authority to solve the problem. Therefore the problem will only weigh them down and cause them to retain knowledge of a person or situation that they can't change. This is wrong.

It's important to check the laws of your state concerning pastoral privilege and confidentiality. I have a friend whose parents are pastors. They worked with a man who had confessed to a crime. Once the authorities found out that this man had done the crime, they sent a subpoena to the pastors to have them testify against this man, figuring that the man had confessed to them. They refused to appear in court as an act of obedience to divine confidentiality. It looked like they were both going to go to prison for refusing to submit to the subpoena. Thank God, the man ended up confessing to the crime so that they wouldn't have to go to prison. However, it became clear that the State of West Virginia did not honor pastoral confidence *(at the time).* Many states do recognize this privilege. However there are guidelines in many states. Some of those guidelines require that a counselor be a licensed or ordained minister. Others require that a counselor be working directly for the licensed or ordained minister.

Pastoral and counseling confidence is vitally important to the health of your ministry and your natural life as well. Taking sensitive information into your own hands could invite God's judgment on you.

I know a former pastoral family who got into great trouble with this very situation. One day, a man in this pastor's church had confessed in great brokenness and despair that he had touched a nephew or relative child sexually. He was devastated, guilty and condemned over the situation and really wanted help. He confessed and begged for forgiveness, help and counsel on what to do to make the situation right again. The pastor helped him and gave him counsel.

This pastor then proceeded to tell his wife of the situation. She works for the State Social Services department. Her day job is to take children away from families who don't deserve to have them in their care. When she heard this confidential information, she immediately took it to her employer and they proceeded to file charges against the young man and have him arrested. She misused the confidential information that her husband ignorantly gave her, and then integrated man's earthly penal system into the divine covering of mercy, deliverance and forgiveness. She brought judgment upon her own household! Three years later, her own husband was in prison for deviate sexual assault on a minor, and they were both removed by God from all pastoral ministry.

Beloved, we stand as ministers and priests of God's divine mercy, grace and forgiveness. We are counselors of restoration and restitution. We are God's spokespersons. We give directions to people to help them out of past sins. We must hold this information confidential at all costs! This is God's governmental pattern. To violate this is to oppose God's mercy and grace that's freely given to all through Christ Jesus.

It is important to also understand that it is not our duty to cover future sin. The hot subject of the time seems to be the abuse of children by priests and ministers as God is exposing and cleaning house of this secret filth. Remember that it is God who's cleaning house, therefore His servants must also clean house.

If you end up in a counseling situation where a habitual child molester, murderer, rapist or abuser of other's rights is confessing to you, you must tell them clearly that you will not be a party to endangering others to future crimes. Your counsel should be biblical, covering, forgiving and restorative in nature. However, many times when a crime has been committed it is important for that person to go to the authorities and make it right by confessing to the crime. This is very cleansing in many cases. You must include these instructions to a habitual criminal.

Be led by the Holy Spirit when counseling special cases, and don't be afraid to ask your spiritual father, your own pastor or mentor for some serious biblical and legal advice if you ever get yourself into a counseling situation that is far beyond the normal session.

THE PROS AND CONS OF STARTING AND MAINTAINING A CHRISTIAN SCHOOL

I honor and respect any ministry that has a Christian school under their care. Schools are a lot of hard work! They require heavy staffing, a lot of T.L.C., finances, equipment, materials, square footage and much more.

Any church or ministry that wants to have a Christian school for children must face the high probability that your church will be subsidizing that school with thousands of dollars every month to keep it functioning properly. Along with those subsidized funds, the school will most likely not be paying great salaries to the teachers and administrators. A Christian school is a merciful operation of extreme love and compassion towards children and their families.

Our church ran a Christian school for three years. We were trained through the producers of the curriculum that we chose and we got off to a good start. We learned quickly that there are many parameters that make your school effective or non-effective, prosperous or impoverished.

1. If parents are not required to participate in the school in some way or another through volunteering their time, they won't have any heart towards helping your school and will look at your ministry as just another "public school" operation that charges them a lot of money.
2. If you don't put a requirement upon the parents for timely payment, many will lag behind and you'll never get paid for school work already completed. You must be willing to be a bill collector. A Christian school

122

operation will quickly learn that many Christians have a hard time paying their bills on time, if ever.

3. If you don't put the tuition fees high enough to subsidize your school, you will suffer financially and the people really won't appreciate your low tuition fees – they'll never say, "Thanks for saving me $100 per month over the other school down the street!".

You will need to weigh out the pros and cons of having a school in your church or ministry before you actually start it up. It's a lot of work *(did I say "a lot"?)* and it's going to cost you money out of your pocket *(did I say, "Cost you money"?)*.

I'm not trying to discourage you from this, but I am saying that you need to heavily seek the Lord on this and do it under a calling from Heaven. It's not good enough to start a Christian school just because you don't like what they're teaching little Johnny down at the public school. For those problems, there's always home school materials – which will save you thousands of dollars per month in subsidies from the church general account.

Again, I admire and praise any church that's taken up the calling to have a Christian school. I encourage every parent to pay the $200 - $500 per month tuition and be thankful that it's not more! They're doing for pennies what the government school would charge dollars to do, and they're doing it in the name of Jesus with a great learning atmosphere of the Holy Spirit, their staff is clearly not there for the money or the career, but for the love and compassion for the children and their rightful Christian upbringing.

YOUTH MINISTRY BUSINESS
"FINDING A YOUTH LEADER"

Finding a youth pastor or youth leader can be very challenging. The job of a youth leader is very demanding because this person many times must do a relational juggling act between the pastor, the church board and the parents. This person must keep them all happy and get something done with the youth at the same time. This can be one of the highest pressure positions, and it's usually given to the person with the least training. *(Did I say that it also pays the least?)*

If the leader of the ministry doesn't cover the youth leader/pastor correctly, this can be a very destructive position for a person to enter into.

I recommend that you find someone that's faithful, available and teachable *(F.A.T.)*. Find someone that can preach the Word of God, develop activities for youth and who has an anointing or ability to draw youth to him/her. God will surface this person if you pray and ask. I recommend having your teens and the parents of the teens pray, seek God and spend quality time asking God to send the right person. When this person does come, they'll be thankful and excited that God has answered prayer. This beats a judgmental attitude from non-praying parents and teens.

When you find your youth leader and commission him/her, make sure that you let them know exactly what you expect. Give them the ground rules in the beginning. Once this is done you must set them free to be creative and build the youth team. Remember that this is delegation of your authority.

There's nothing worse than feeling the pressure of parents and unruly teens bearing on a youth leader, and knowing also that the pastor is not standing with that same youth leader.

I fully recommend that you have monthly meetings with your youth leader. Encourage, instruct, build him up, give creative ideas and wisdom that she needs from her leader. When an issue arises with a parent, a teen or an elder, do your best to stand with the youth leader. Don't allow them to be shot at by blood thirst congregational members who just want to judge or shoot someone. If your youth leader is taking shots, those who are doing the shooting are actually shooting at you. The principle of authority is found when the people complained against Moses. God told Moses to step aside because the people were complaining about God himself. Don't let the people shoot at your youth leader, as they're actually attacking you and God Himself.

Stand with your youth leader! Rebuke him in private if he needs it and stand with her in public. Let the people see that the two of you are a rock solid wall of agreement for the love of God and your youth. This will strengthen your youth leader, the youth of the group, and the parents who respect authority. They will see that their teens are honestly safe with your ministry.

Once your youth leader is in place, give him room to build and plan. She's not going to do it the way that you would, so don't demand that of her. They don't talk the same, wear the same clothes, watch the same programs or listen to the same style of music. Let God use your youth leader in a new and creative way and support it with all you have.

Encourage your youth leader to get involved with youth trips and fellowship, youth camps, evangelistic campaigns and local, inter-state and international missions trips. It's also my recommendation that you encourage your youth leader to get your teens involved with inter-church youth functions, active relationships with other youth pastors in the community, rallies and activities. Be community minded and always push for *"unity"* in the community. There's nothing much worse than for a pure hearted youth leader wanting to build relationships with other youth pastors and youth groups, only to find that he has hit a huge wall of separation that's been built by their adult church leader(s). He won't be able to walk in unity of the Spirit, and can't shake hands with the other wonderful youth leaders of the community. This wall of separation will *"discourage and dismantle"* the growth potential and reproductive strength of your youth ministry.

Make sure that you determine early on which kind of youth ministry that you want. There are two types of youth ministry in my opinion, and they are either *"youth groups"* or *"youth ministries"*. *"Youth groups"* are shepherd/pastoral themed and have a purpose to gather teens together to instruct them in the Word of God and Christian fellowship. However, *"youth ministry"* purpose is apostolic themed and has an *"outreach and sending"* focus and a purpose of training young people into ministry-styled lifestyle. *(For more information of "apostolic themed ministry, see chapter three – "God's New Testament Governing Structure")*

Determining the focus of your youth program early on will help you to choose and direct the right youth leader. These youth leader styles will be distinctively different in their priorities and capabilities.

There are more youth ministry resources available on our website at www.basicsforsuccess.com .

MINISTRY TIP:
A ministry who is honestly interested in the next generation will designate money and resources into that youth ministry.

Lu. 12:34 For where your treasure is, there will your heart be also.

INSURANCE & PROTECTION

We live in a day where some people live like brute beasts. They will create opportunity to extort money from your ministry. This includes using their children, youth or elderly momma to get into a financial lawsuit with you. It has happened more than you would ever believe.

It's important to discuss this subject with your youth leader(s) and volunteers. You need to have proper insurance for your ministry with an umbrella of protection that covers you and any worker wherever you're at. A good insurance policy will protect any of you, wherever you're at, and whatever you're doing. If you're at the mall in the name of your ministry, you're covered. If you're driving down the road with a car load of young people, you're covered. If anything at all goes wrong, you're covered. If your youth leader is counseling a teen who later commits suicide, you're covered.

Whenever you take the youth on a trip of any kind, make sure that you have parental release and medical treatment forms filled out for every youth that gets into the vehicle. Make solid policy decisions that no one gets in the vehicle without these permission slips signed. Failure to have your bases covered with proper insurance and parental release forms could literally be the death of your ministry.

Money hungry, lawsuit happy people would just love to see their child in an accident. They'd love to see you make a mistake with their loved one. They'd be happy to find you liable for an action that will land you in court. If you're not protected, your church could be writing a one million dollar check *(or more)* to cover a court case. Just defending yourself against a lawsuit could cost you $50,000 or more in attorney fees. Are you prepared to write that check? Get yourself adequately covered! This is part of protecting and overseeing your God-given ministry.

Make sure that you have your entire ministry covered with regards to legal documents, parental permission slips, disclaimers and proper insurance coverage. In this day and age of law suits and money hungry wolves, you must have your ministry well covered with church, counseling, umbrella, auto and property insurance. Seek the best companies who can help you to be secure against enemy attack on your calling and ministry. Church insurance doesn't have to be expensive. Don't be caught without it!

See our web site for more resources to help you with your insurance needs.

YOUTH RESOURCES

Youth ministry is ever changing as generations change. Use the internet to find the ministries that God is anointing for the day and pattern your youth ministry after them. From skateboard parks, TV ministry, bands and concerts, youth centers, multi-media ministry, drama teams and more, youth ministry is ever expanding and changing to meet the current needs of our young generation. On our website, we have links to other powerful ministries and youth ministry help sites. One of my favorite sites is loaded with tons of free ministry business information, parental permission slips, teen games, ideas and other great youth ministry elements. Go to www.successforlife.com and get this free information.

NETWORKING RELATIONSHIPS FOR INCREASE

The rich and wealthy of this world will tell you that networking is the key to extreme success and prosperity. Large teams of people who come together to do a large task are the same teams who are able to build empires and make billions of dollars.

However, we've not totally figured that out in the local church. Many leaders have trouble getting just a few of their people to come together as a team to accomplish a little task. Most of them don't realize that their people are only reflecting the leader's own stand within the Christian community.

Many churches have been trained to be alone, to stand in survival mode, to operate autonomous of one another, and to keep to their own business. That's why these churches will always be small in their thinking and vision, and why they will never reach their city in a big way. Every leader has to wake up at one point or another and realize that he/she can't reach our city alone. He can't impact the world on his own, and she can't multiply relationships with Christ unless there's other people involved to multiply.

Many leaders are being challenged at this very moment by God to lay down their personal agendas, scrap their covert plans of building a little support kingdom for their ministry, and to expand their vision to God's vision.

Isa 55:8 For my thoughts are not your thoughts, neither are your ways my ways, saith the LORD.
Isa 55:9 For as the heavens are higher than the earth, so are my ways higher than your ways, and my thoughts than your thoughts.

God has commanded in New Testament government order that the church be united together as many members of one body, deeply in need and in communication with one another to the degree that when one suffers, we all suffer. However, churches today are associated only with their denominations rather than with the body of Christ. They are drawn away in self-taught fear, staying away from other churches that they don't understand. Leaders don't like the looks of another ministry or they don't like it's smell, not realizing that they're looking at a *"foot"* in the body of Christ, and a ministry that they deeply need if they're going to take a step in their city successfully together.

Still other leaders who have eye ministries will judge other less desirable looking ministries and will be guilty of saying, *"I have no need of that ministry or that leader in relationship."*

(1 Cor 12:20 – 27) But now are they many members, yet but one body. And the eye cannot say unto the hand, I have no need of thee: nor again the head to the feet, I have no need of you. Nay, much more those members of the body, which seem to be more feeble, are necessary: And those members of the body, which we think to be less honourable, upon these we bestow more abundant honour; and our uncomely parts have more abundant comeliness. For our comely parts have no need: but God hath tempered the body together, having given more abundant honour to that part which lacked: That there should be no schism in the body; but that the members should have the same care one for another. And whether one member suffer, all the members suffer with it; or one member be honoured, all the members rejoice with it. Now ye are the body of Christ, and members in particular.

If we ever discover the power in God's New Testament command to come together, and realize the need that we have for one another, the church will take over the world in end-time harvest like we've never known before!

It took John D. Rockefeller fifteen years to become a billionaire through networking and building of the oil distribution system to get oil from the ground into your gas tank.

It took Bill Gates approximately ten years to become a billionaire by using IBM's network to grow rapidly.

It took Michael Dell (Dell Computers) and Steve Case (Founder of AOL) less than five years to become billionaires, and they each did it by tapping into the power of networking.

Beloved, it's taking people less and less time to achieve enormous goals because of the power of networking. We live in the information age where it's possible to network at exponential rates. The world is networking all around us and is virtually laying network cable under, above and around our churches. Yet, we can't seem to network our abilities with the church that's just down the street, let alone with all of the churches in town. This ought not be, and the problem smells of a covert satanic plot to divide and conquer the destinies of God's great men and women of God.

I've always been a networking person. Anything significant that I've ever done for God was done through networking of relationships. As a matter of fact, God showed me a great concept in 1986 when I launched *"Youth Network"*. This network was the theme of my youth ministry for years, and ended up developing into an international youth television program called, *"Youth Network TV"*.

While in prayer for the youth ministry one day in 1986, the Lord showed me a vision of a large fishing net and also a single rope. I began to focus on the fishing net rather than the single rope. The net was made up of multiple *"single"* ropes, but the strength of the net was in the knotted or tied segments of rope. With these strong ties, the many ropes became one net, a net that would work. It was in the strength of this multi-roped net that God would bring in an end-time harvest of fish. However, a single rope line would only bring in one fish at a time. Then I saw the Master pull up on this fishing net, and multitudes of young people were caught in this net just like fish would be.

I realized that this vision I was seeing was in direct relation to *"Networking"* of ministry relationships. I saw that the only community strength that the church has is dependant upon our inter-church relationships with one another. I began to envision every church and youth ministry in our city coming together and *"networking"*. I saw that if this could be successfully done, the youth of our city would never be able to escape the *"network"* of the church. The network of relationship would totally surround a young person, even in their time of temptation, running, back

131

sliding or struggle. The fish would be successfully caught without the ability to escape.

I immediately came up with the phrase *"Youth Network", the Net that will Work!"* Since that time I have attempted to network with other ministries, churches and youth ministries, building lasting relationships. I must admit that quite frequently, I've been met with very strong walls of resistance built by fearful and judgmental ministers. I have not been totally successful, but I still believe in the network of relationships, and I know that God is calling for all ministries to inter-relate past their former walls of denomination, position, territory and personal comfort.

Imagine with me for a moment.... a single city church made up of smaller church cells with no pre-determined walls, no divisions and no barriers with one another. *(Believers in Christ)*

Imagine.... a network of pastors, ministers and Christians who are tolerant with one another and who are mature enough to actualize the fact that we're all members of the body of Christ.

Imagine.... being actively needed by the other churches in your community.

Imagine.... the networking of your actual strengths and giftings with the great need that the other churches have for those gifts.

Imagine.... the areas of your great need being fulfilled because other churches and ministries are giving into your active need.

Imagine.... your church congregation learning from the you that networking of multi-denominations is good, and their relationships begin to increase towards other church people while their fears of those *"other"* churches decrease.

Imagine.... a church that actually starts acting like a family rather than different nations and people groups.

132

Is this spiritual network actually possible in our day? It's highly unlikely unless church leaders get an image in their hearts of the life, power and destiny that will unfold with this newly networked unity in Christ. Leaders are going to have to dismantle old, generational stone walls that our forefathers built. We're going to have to drop our contentious and critical spirits towards our brothers in Christ. We must become tolerant with Christ and His body rather than judgmental of the other churches that He has called into our city. We're going to have to drop our pride and arrogance, come into humility and repentance, and embrace God's heart for networking.

(Phil 2:2 KJV) Fulfil ye my joy, that ye be likeminded, having the same love, being of one accord, of one mind.

(Eph 5:21 KJV) Submitting yourselves one to another in the fear of God.

Remember, the only strength that the church of Jesus Christ has in your city will be found in the relationships between pastors, church leaders, and the church body at large. Divisive, solo, lone-ranger ministries are a thing of the past. But a noble minister/servant with the heart of God will seek to promote unity among the brethren, and will fight to preserve relationships among church leaders.

God is building a net in your area. This net will work. However, the strength of the net is the *"knot"* of strong relationship that your rope/ministry has with other church leaders that have come across your rope's path.

Aren't you thankful for the successful network of relationships that are holding your own natural body together today? The very nerve, chemical and electrical network has allowed you to live, breath and move successfully. This can happen in the church world with our participation!

The Business Of Ministry

(Eph 5:30 KJV) For we are members of his body, of his flesh, and of his bones.

It's true that there will be those who join the network for selfish motivation. Some will use and abuse you. Some will need time to learn about brotherhood and relationships being a two way street. There will be need for patience, mercy, instruction and humility rather than offence. The Spirit of God will help you to walk in love, forgiveness, perseverance and patience while He instructs the other brethren. No, it's not going to be easy, but it is going to be important for destiny's sake in your city and ministry.

Again, the principle of mission first, team second, Individual third comes into play. God's mission needs to be fulfilled at the highest priority. His mission is one of bringing the body of Christ together for building up unto a perfect man.

The best time that you can spend this year will be networking with other ministries, churches and leaders. Offer your services and strengths to other churches who need them. Don't demand anything from these people, but serve them. Give of yourself into the network, build the network, trust the network and honor the network. The network that I'm talking about is the living body of Christ with each important part linked, networked and serving a greater purpose.

Seek God to find the powerful secret of networking. When you find this secret, your ministry, vision and focus will change forever. You will never be locked into small thinking and nano mindsets again.

Remember who's Kingdom we're building. It is God who commands that we honor one another and network in relationship. This is good and pleasing and it produces anointing that is not available otherwise.

The Business Of Ministry

(Psa 133:1 – 3) A Song of degrees of David. Behold, how good and how pleasant it is for brethren to dwell together in unity! It is like the precious ointment upon the head, that ran down upon the beard, even Aaron's beard: that went down to the skirts of his garments; As the dew of Hermon, and as the dew that descended upon the mountains of Zion: for there the LORD commanded the blessing, even life for evermore.

I met a wonderful man who's helped build an AIDS Dream Center Hospital in Durban, S. Africa. He stated that their only struggle in helping AIDS patients there is the lack of association and networking with other churches Many of them won't get involved or even speak to him about their community AIDS problem *(one million at present have AIDS symptoms in that one city!)*. He said this great statement that caused me to step back and pray.

"Every day, church leaders are building towards a kingdom. It's a shame to find that not many of these kingdoms actually lead to God's Kingdom."

The secret to networking is vital to every ministry leader in the world. If we ever master this secret, our cities will be won for Christ in a very short time, to the honor and glory of God. No man will be boasting in his own leadership capabilities, but all will be pointing to Christ who is the head of the body/team/army.

Make sure that the kingdom that you're building leads to God's. The best way is to give yourself wholly to networking and serving other member churches and ministries in the body.

(Rev 11:15) And the seventh angel sounded; and there were great voices in heaven, saying, The kingdoms of this world are become the kingdoms of our Lord, and of his Christ; and he shall reign for ever and ever.

Oh how I long to see the manifestation on earth of the seventh angel's sound and the decree of Heaven's great voices!

135

DISFELLOWSHIP OR REMOVING OF A PERSON OR FAMILY FROM YOUR MINISTRY

There comes a time in every minister's life when you are faced with a rebellious, anti-Christ spirited person or family that threatens to divide, split or destroy your ministry. The person might walk in a powerful Jezebel spirit, or might have a strong relational control over some of your people. They may have become hostile in their actions. No matter what you do to try to pacify, help, counsel or lead these people, they are non-teachable and become a threat to God's ministry and His people. These types of people are everywhere in the body of Christ. Because of a tremendous, widespread lack of biblical instruction on how to deal with these people, there is rampant destruction that moves through the body of Christ at an alarming rate. However, this should not be! Many leaders have not understood or withstood these types of people with a sound doctrinal New Testament governmental stand.

2 Tim 3:2 For men shall be lovers of their own selves, covetous, boasters, proud, blasphemers, disobedient to parents, unthankful, unholy,
(2 Tim 3:3 – 9) Without natural affection, trucebreakers, false accusers, incontinent, fierce, despisers of those that are good, Traitors, heady, highminded, lovers of pleasures more than lovers of God; Having a form of godliness, but denying the power thereof: from such turn away. For of this sort are they which creep into houses, and lead captive silly women laden with sins, led away with divers lusts, Ever learning, and never able to come to the knowledge of the truth. Now as Jannes and Jambres withstood Moses, so do these also resist the truth: men of corrupt minds, reprobate concerning the faith. But they shall proceed no further: for their folly shall be manifest unto all men, as theirs also was.

2 Timothy clearly states that these types of men will have the form of godliness, but they're resisters of the truth and they're reprobate concerning the faith. These men must be exposed and

136

pointed out to the people of God. This requires strong leadership, and not many men have had the tenacity, biblical training or assurance to go head to head with this "level of devil" so to speak.

God repeatedly went head to head with Israel. He had to deal with their sin and rebellion. He dealt with Israel with a firm hand of correction in order to bring Israel to repentance, and to return to their covenant with him. God turned apostate Israel over to their enemies repeatedly in order to teach them not to rebel and serve other gods.

(Judg 10:6 – 7) And the children of Israel did evil again in the sight of the LORD, and served Baalim, and Ashtaroth, and the gods of Syria, and the gods of Zidon, and the gods of Moab, and the gods of the children of Ammon, and the gods of the Philistines, and forsook the LORD, and served not him. And the anger of the LORD was hot against Israel, and he sold them into the hands of the Philistines, and into the hands of the children of Ammon.

This is simply one of many times that the Lord turned Israel over to their enemies to chastise and correct them. This is the way that God has always worked, and so He continues to this day. Through His church leadership He turns people over to shame and separation in order to bring them to true repentance, and cause them to seek and accept Jesus Christ as their savior and Lord. God is longsuffering and He doesn't just jump into turning His people over. However, there comes a divine time when a man or woman stops listening to God's voice and to the instruction or warnings of the church leadership. It's at this time when church governmental action is required.

Titus tells us that a divisive person must be warned, but only twice. If they don't heed the two warnings, then three strikes – you're out! The scripture commands the church to have nothing to do with such a person because he is warped, full of sin and

self condemned, not knowing anything about the sacrifice of
Jesus Christ or the power of God unto salvation.

*(NIV Titus 3:10 - 11) Warn a divisive person once, and then
warn him a second time. After that, have nothing to do with him.
You may be sure that such a man is warped and sinful; he is self-
condemned.*

*(KJV Titus 3:10 - 11) A man that is an heretic after the first and
second admonition reject; Knowing that he that is such is
subverted, and sinneth, being condemned of himself.*

How many divisive people do you know that are running
rampant in the church today. How about in your own ministry?
Have they been sternly warned once? Twice? Have they been
removed from the church and the people taught to have nothing
to do with these types of people? If not, then the power of the
New Testament covenant is not in operation in that ministry.

Are these people supposed to be given two chances "per
church"? Then if they don't respond correctly, should the
church leadership send them on down the road to just do it
again? While the church leadership may be relieved that this
trouble has left their church, did they even consider which
church was now going to inherit that problem? Most times the
answer is "no". As a matter of fact, most of the problems that
you inherited in your ministry have come from other ministries
who didn't even bother to warn you about these new problem
people. If you had been fore-warned, things might have turned
out differently. Many churches wouldn't have allowed these
people into their committees, on the worship team or teaching in
the Sunday school class before finding out that they have a
divisive devil on their hands. If only someone would have
warned them.

The thought that we can send a problem on down the road to
another church can be very hurtful. This mentality wreaks of
selfishness and minimized vision, and certainly does not promote

the body of Christ as a whole. These nano-mindsets must be wrenched from our ministries and leadership.

Would you send a rabid dog down through your neighborhood which is full of playing children? Just as long as that dog doesn't come into your yard, it's OK, right? Wrong! What you know can save many people from pain, destruction and division. Don't ever be guilty of simple minded, selfish thinking. The mission of God requires our obedience well beyond the small 4 walls of our little churches.

When church leadership begins to rise up and exercise New Testament authority against the spirit of division, many walls will fall in the body of Christ and a great cleansing of the church will take place. Hopefully those who are divisive will come to a knowledge of repentance and will turn away from their wicked scheming and divisive activities that tear down the body of Christ and the work of God.

Paul dealt with a man in Corinth who was having a sexual relationship with his father's mother. He dealt with this man in New Testament biblical order.

(1 Cor 5:1 – 5) It is reported commonly that there is fornication among you, and such fornication as is not so much as named among the Gentiles, that one should have his father's wife. And ye are puffed up, and have not rather mourned, that he that hath done this deed might be taken away from among you. For I verily, as absent in body, but present in spirit, have judged already, as though I were present, concerning him that hath so done this deed, In the name of our Lord Jesus Christ, when ye are gathered together, and my spirit, with the power of our Lord Jesus Christ, To deliver such an one unto Satan for the destruction of the flesh, that the spirit may be saved in the day of the Lord Jesus.

Paul was appalled at the open sinful activities that this man was involved in. He couldn't believe that this man carried out this

139

sin while continuing in fellowship among the believers. Even more than that, he confronted the pride and disobedience of the church leadership for not taking hard line action against this man. He commanded that the man be handed over to Satan for the destruction of his flesh, so that somehow – his spirit may be saved in the day of the Lord. He literally commanded Satan to begin eating on the flesh of this man in hopes that he would stop sinning and come to repentance.

When is the last time you heard of a present day church leader handing a person in their church over to Satan for the destruction of their flesh? Can you remember a church service where this happened? Can you *EVER* remember hearing of such a thing in today's New Testament church? In the day of seeker sensitive services and happiness hype, such an activity would never be allowed in many churches. This action has been given to the New Testament church for ultimate correction of an individual. Yet, only strong leaders will dare to trust God's New Testament commands and enact His Word in these situations. This takes humility and trust in God's Word, rather than fear of the people and their opinions.

What if the apostle Peter walked in the fear of the people? Would he have dared to deliver the Word of the Lord to Annanias and Saphira on the day when the New Testament Holy Spirit killed them for lying?

(Acts 5:9) Then Peter said unto her, How is it that ye have agreed together to tempt the Spirit of the Lord? Behold, the feet of them which have buried thy husband are at the door, and shall carry thee out.

This doesn't make for a great day of church growth and it doesn't make the seeker sensitive person want to come back to church there. However, it does fulfill the mandate of God for the New Testament, and it causes a holy fear and respect to come upon all of the people. Submission to this New Testament command is also the gateway for many signs, wonders and miracles to be performed by the apostles and ministry gifts of the church.

(Acts 5:11 – 12) And great fear came upon all the church, and upon as many as heard these things. And by the hands of the apostles were many signs and wonders wrought among the people; (and they were all with one accord in Solomon's porch).

It's important to note that it was the apostles who exercised great authority in the Ananias & Saphira story, the man caught in fornication with his father's wife and the divisive man. Apostolic authority is being radically restored to the church in this day and age, and with it comes the faith and grace to deal with open sin and rebellion in the house of God.

It's not in the grace gifting of most pastors to be able to exact this type of governmental procedure within their church alone. The five fold ministry giftings are vitally needed to accomplish this undertaking. That's why many pastors can't, won't or refuse to exact this New Testament authority which is commanded by God within His church. This is also why many signs and wonders are not present in today's churches, as the gateway of obedience is closed and governmental authority is not in place largely in the church .

It's vital to operate in extreme humility and love when activating these governmental decisions within the church. A prideful and arrogant heart will cause you to become ensnared by the same sins.

(Gal 6:1) Brethren, if a man be overtaken in a fault, ye which are spiritual, restore such an one in the spirit of meekness; considering thyself, lest thou also be tempted.

Satan is looking for a way into your life. Haughtiness, arrogance and pride will give you a double portion of the judgment you just exacted upon an unrepentant man. I say this with great fear and respect for the process, as I know first hand how the devil would

141

like to sift those who must judge according to God's New Testament government plan.

Paul commands us not to associate with any so called brother in Christ who is sexually immoral, greedy, involved in slander, a drunk or a swindler of money. We are commanded not to even eat with such individuals. Paul then tells us to expel the wicked person from among us. However, the restaurants are filled every Sunday with Christians who eat and drink with the best of open sinners, they themselves falling into the sins of slander, greed and other kinds of evil that pull good saints down.

(1 Cor 5:11- 13) But now I am writing you that you must not associate with anyone who calls himself a brother but is sexually immoral or greedy, an idolater or a slanderer, a drunkard or a swindler. With such a man do not even eat. What business is it of mine to judge those outside the church? Are you not to judge those inside? God will judge those outside. "Expel the wicked man from among you."

When was the last time you heard your pastor tell you to not associate with Mr. XYZ because he's involved in swindling of funds, sexual immorality or greed? When was the last time you heard your spiritual leaders actually warn you in public to stay away from Mr. XYZ because he's unrepentant and dangerous to the body of Christ and the work of God? This will never happen in a "would be" hyper-friendly, happy church where everything's fine and perfect.

Jesus gave a four-step New Testament process in dealing with someone who sins against you.

(Mat 18:15 – 20) Moreover if thy brother shall trespass against thee, go and tell him his fault between thee and him alone: if he shall hear thee, thou hast gained thy brother. But if he will not hear thee, then take with thee one or two more, that in the mouth of two or three witnesses every word may be established. And if he shall neglect to hear them, tell it unto the church: but if he

142

neglect to hear the church, let him be unto thee as a heathen man and a publican. Verily I say unto you, Whatsoever ye shall bind on earth shall be bound in heaven: and whatsoever ye shall loose on earth shall be loosed in heaven. Again I say unto you, that if two of you shall agree on earth as touching any thing that they shall ask, it shall be done for them of my Father which is in heaven. For where two or three are gathered together in my name, there am I in the midst of them.

1. Go to the brother and attempt to work out the sin issue personally, one on one.
2. Take one or two Christian friends along and try once again to correct the sinful situation so that the problem is resolved.
3. Take the man before the entire church body and tell them all what the man has done, in hope that he will hear the voice of the church correcting him and that he will repent of his actions.
4. Change your relationship with this man from a brother to a publican and a sinner. His sin has shown him for who he really is. He's a non-believer and is hard-hearted and wicked. The only message that this man needs to begin to hear form the church is one of repentance of his works, and salvation from sin and dead works through the spilled blood of Jesus Christ.

Jesus gives to the church, binding authority and the authority to loose a person in heaven and earth. He declares that whenever two or more of us are in agreement that it will be done, and that he will stand in our midst to judge in accord with our judgment.

This is heavy New Testament stuff. This is Heaven's correctional system that God has instituted in the church of the Lord Jesus Christ. He has commanded us to learn about this system, humble ourselves as servants, and be willing to stand up and exact this governmental process when needed to protect the body of Christ and the family of God. It's not a pleasant thing to do, but for the love of God and His church, it's the highest form of love that a leader can walk in, to protect the church of God.

*Remember the priority of **Mission, Team, Individual** from chapter 6 Staff Help - Policy Manual.* The mission is top priority, then the team, then the individual. No mission is worth losing because of an individual who decides to move in destructive, hateful behavior and arrogance.

I want to clarify once again that governmental action of this sort should be entered into with fear and trembling, as we are commanded to judge these situations, but if we judge with pride and arrogance, we will become guilty of the same crimes and the grace of God will be pulled from our lives so that we might understand the humility that is necessary to judge in New Testament governmental order.

I would like to share a story with you concerning this governmental order and how I saw this order in operation through my spiritual father, an apostle of Jesus Christ.

Years ago, I was the youth pastor at a small church in the mid-West. There was a long time family stronghold in that church that continually attempted to raise it's head against our pastor and leadership team. That spirit would operate through some of the long time family members who had helped to establish that church. On one occasion, my pastor was being fought so hard by one of the ladies *(family members)* of the church, that he began to warn her to stop her evil scheming, divisive conversation and abusive control. He warned her twice. She persisted in open defiance to his warnings. One day in the middle of the week, he was putting up with another verbal abuse and Jezebel thrash session, and he'd had enough. He told her, *"I'm no longer your pastor. As a matter of fact, you've become so defiant and divisive that I'm handing you over to Satan for the destruction of your flesh."* She stormed out of the room in pride and arrogance and vowed to never return to the church.

The Business Of Ministry

Immediately that day, her hands began to curl up and she came down with a crippling case of carpal tunnel which caused her to not be able to work. Her two children who were somewhere around 8 – 12 years old both came down with intense blisters and boils all over their bodies. They went to the doctor but could find no relief of their symptoms as nothing would work to take the sores away. After about two weeks of intense pain, joblessness and family trauma, the lady came back to my pastor humbled and repentant. She begged for his forgiveness and asked him to pray for her. My mercy-filled pastor accepted her back into the sheep fold, spoke forgiveness over her and prayed for her. The carpal tunnel and the children's blisters left immediately and she was restored by the hand of God through New Testament governmental operation. This operation struck a holy fear in our church members.

A CRAZY STORY OF SIN IN THE CHURCH

When I moved to St. Louis, MO in 1993, we had met a man from the area who was pastoring a church and wanted to merge or transition his church into ours. He was coming up to a trial on state charges of child sex abuse. He was positioning his church for the worst. He had a great group of beloved people, and they were all convinced of his innocence. I personally went to his attorney with him and the attorney told me that this was a trumped up case with no evidence to substantiate the two teen boy's claims of repeated sexual assault. I had always been told that a man in America was innocent until proven guilty. Our church decided to stand with this pastor, who absolutely claimed innocence through the entire ramp-up to the trial. The people in the church mortgaged their homes for his defense fund and people gave inheritance money and savings accounts. My wife and I personally pulled out every dollar from our savings account to help this man pay for his legal defense. Our church found ourselves praying one thing. "Lord, let the truth be brought out

145

and expose the lie!" We didn't realize that God's will included exposing a lie in the church, which would soon be revealed.

A few months later, the trial of the decade began against this man. I sat in the court room and watched the evidence unfold, putting this man in multiple ungodly situations with different boys, in gay zones in homo-sexual infested public parks, in the homosexual bar zones, and renting pornography from shops in his area. The evidence against him was overwhelming. Despite the defense's attempt to bring character witnesses, the pastor's wife, his friends and even the pastor's testimony himself, the jury threw the book at this man and convicted him quickly on multiple counts of deviate sexual assault. This blew my mind, to say the least. I had been lied to by a pastor.

The man was led off to jail to await sentencing in a community that was ready to lynch him right there at the trial. All of this man's church members were at the trial and they blindly wept and asked me, *"Why did God allow this innocent man to be convicted? We prayed for truth to come out and he's now in jail!"*

I launched an investigation of my own because I was deeply disturbed in my spirit. After some digging, I found out that many of this man's character witnesses *(mostly young men and boys)* had been told to lie on the stand for this pastor, at all costs. I found another young man who confessed that this man had sexually abused him since he was just a young boy. I found that multiple other churches through the years had fired him and just removed him from their churches without proper Kingdom governmental action.

NOTE: None of these churches ever contacted one another to warn of this man's unrepentant behavior, and many would suffer in the future because of their individualist church government mentalities of just sending their problems on down the road.

After talking with his wife, she also confessed that she lied on the witness stand to cover up his double lifestyle. My pastor and I both set a plan of action to attempt to restore the victims of the crime, the people who'd lied in a court of law, and the pastor who needed a miracle in his life, restoration, healing, counsel and a huge shot of mercy from a very angry judge who would be sentencing him soon.

I got a miraculous pass to see this man in jail when no one else was allowed to see him. I told him what I'd found out and that I knew that he was guilty. I told him that our prayers had been fulfilled when we asked God to bring out the truth and expose the lie. I told him that he needed to confess to his crime and ask God and the people that he had lied to, to forgive him. He must ask the victims of the crimes to forgive him, and to throw himself at the mercy of the courts and ask them for help with his sin, disease and criminal behavior. However, he cold-heartedly told me that if he were to confess to anything, it would shut down his opportunity for an appeal. *"APPEAL?"* He wanted an appeal? He wanted to drag those young, wounded victims back onto the stand, and as a pastor, supposedly standing for and preaching the truth, he was going to call those victims liars? He was going to try to manipulate the system because of his pride and get off on a technicality?

I approached him once again with the assistance and support of four spiritual leaders who were a part of his ministry life. I told him that he had no choice but to confess to God, the people in his church and to the victims. This was God's way. These people had now been integrated into my church and they were all suffering intensely because they believed that this man was innocent, because he promised them that he was. However, the man told me that he wouldn't do it. I went to him for a third time and pressured him with the eldership of our church and four outside ministry leaders. I gave him a date to confess in writing, or I'd tell the church myself what he had done and all that I knew in an attempt to shame him into confessing and repenting. At that point, he threw some strange, so-called prophetic statement at me indicating that the Lord wanted to match up some dates before he were to confess, so he was asking for a few more weeks so the dates could line up. *"What was that?"* I never heard of the Lord telling us to wait to repent until the dates line up.

This man never repented, so as I had promised, I brought him before the entire church. His wife had become belligerent towards us also, so I took her before the church as well and told them about the lies, deceptions and other sins that this man had committed with the other boy. I told the church that I was giving him and his wife one week to repent publicly or that our governing eldership would be forced to hand this man over to Satan for the destruction of his flesh so that his spirit may be saved in the day of the Lord.

The man quickly counted me as one of his enemies and his wife joined his side. They never repented of their sin, therefore our church eldership and ministry team joined together in the presence of the Lord one Sunday and we handed those people over to Satan for the destruction of their flesh. We commanded our people to not eat with them and to treat them as non-believers. We told our people to preach the gospel of salvation to them if they ever saw them again, as that is the gospel that this family needed to hear and receive.

Just weeks after this action, the man was sentenced to 156 years of prison time. The heated judge had no place in his court for an unrepentant pastor who used his calling to prey on young boys. He was diagnosed as HIV positive and then began to serve his prison sentence. He attempted to get an appeal trial to overturn his conviction a few years later, but one of his old staff members came forward who lied once for him on the stand. This person said, *"I won't lie for him again."* This new convincing evidence destroyed his chance for an appeal trial. Still, this man ended up serving a minimized negotiated sentence and is out free today.

This man has served in multiple ministries and those ministries have suffered intensely to this day. Some of these ministries have been told of our New Testament governmental action. Some have believed that they could side step New Testament governmental order and work with this man any way. They've only hurt their own ministries in the long run. Only those who bind and loose with New Testament governmental authority can reverse the process. This man will have to come back to the source in order to have the process reversed. Before a reversal will take place, he will confess, repent, restore and make full restitution to the very best of his ability. This is the simplicity of Christ's message.

I wish that I could tell you that he had repented and come to the truth, but the fact remains that he is still using his strong and powerful influence on people to imitate a godly man. He has worked for different ministries and is still working with young boys under the same method of operation. We have see him from time to time at a gas station or grocery store with a young boy along side.

If this man had gone God's way, we found out that he'd have been out of prison in 9 months. With a confession, the judge would have sentenced him to a 9 month rehabilitation program for confessed child molesters. If he would have confessed, he would have been embraced by a very loving group of sheep, his family would have been cared for while he was serving his sentence, and he would have had many friends in ministry that would have supported him financially and spiritually. He'd be in active fellowship today (years later) and would probably be restored and back in some sort of church-help function *(away from young boys)* with a bright future ahead of him.

As it stands, this man must forever dodge the governmental decision that was exacted against him by an apostolic ministry who walked in obedience to God's command. He will forever have to run and hide, fabricate stories and lie to cover up the truth. Until he humbles himself, repents and confesses his sin, until he brings restitution to those that he's stolen from, there will be no opportunity for him to ever succeed or prosper in the Kingdom of God. I personally fear for his soul. I know that liars, abusers, thieves and sexually immoral people cannot enter the Kingdom of Heaven. My prayers persist for his salvation.

(1 Cor 6:9 KJV) Know ye not that the unrighteous shall not inherit the kingdom of God? Be not deceived: neither fornicators, nor idolaters, nor adulterers, nor effeminate, nor abusers of themselves with mankind,
(1 Cor 6:10 KJV) Nor thieves, nor covetous, nor drunkards, nor revilers, nor extortioners, shall inherit the kingdom of God.

Not long ago, we found that this man had worked his way into an associate pastor position in the mid-West. We couldn't believe it! How did he do this? I prayed to the Lord and asked, "Lord, should I call these people and tell them what this man's about?" We felt that we were to only pray for this man to be revealed and exposed for who he really is. Nevertheless, some of his old time victims found out that he was pastoring again and called in the local newspaper reporters on him. Because of the new and revealing news, he's no longer pastoring for that ministry, and that ministry took the heat publicly in the news for bringing him on board.

I have to say the story doesn't end here. When we handed this man and his wife over to Satan for the destruction of their flesh years ago, we followed up on them. They had joined a predominant church and when he got out of prison, he began hanging out with their young boys. I made multiple calls for the pastor to contact me immediately on an issue of grave importance. After multiple calls, the pastor never called me back. In a last effort, I sent a multiple page letter outlining in detail what I have told you (and more). I told him of the lies, deceit and the secret unrepentant lifestyle of this man. I warned him not to receive this man into their ministry as he had been dis-fellowshipped from the body of Christ. He had to repent and make restitution in a very large way. I faxed this letter onto the pastor's personal secretary's desk with priority. I never heard from the pastor, though I begged him for a return phone call. This is a pure example of how the church at large knows nothing about God's New Testament governmental process.

Can you imagine how many young boys have been exposed in that church to an HIV positive child predator? I say this not to condemn the church, but to expose a tremendous deficit in the church that must be corrected in obedience to God! Oh, that all of our churches would operate in New Testament governmental order and authority! If so, this man would have never found a resting place to lay his head, and would have to decide once and for all whether or not he wants to live for the King of kings, or for the devil. He'd have no place to hide. As it stands, he's found a perfect place to hide his sin, right in the unschooled local church.

I told you this horror story so that you would know that these stories exist in every city and in many churches. One of these stories is coming your way sooner or later, and you've got to be armed with New Testament governmental order to be able to protect God's vision, the team and the individual. The church-body deserves shepherds who will raise their staff against wolves in sheep's clothing!

Lastly, I need to mention that there's been other churches and ministries who thought that our church body were crazy with this "handing over to Satan" thing. They didn't recognize the power of binding and losing (Matt. 18:18, 19), and they stood in ignorance or arrogance assuming that they could handle this man and his wife when they received them into their churches. However, this sort of reception is just like the ship who received Jonah on their way to Joppa. Trouble lies ahead for any ignorant or arrogant church body who thinks that they can over-ride New Testament apostolic decree. As a matter of fact, the only one who can typically *"loose"* a person from binding New Testament decree is the one who *"bound"* and issued the decree in the first place.

151

The Business Of Ministry

Mat 18:18 Verily I say unto you, Whatsoever ye shall bind on earth shall be bound in heaven: and whatsoever ye shall loose on earth shall be loosed in heaven.
Mat 18:19 Again I say unto you, That if two of you shall agree on earth as touching any thing that they shall ask, it shall be done for them of my Father which is in heaven.

God commands that a man goes to the one whom he sins against and make restitution. You can't just go on down the road and decide that you're repented at a later time and a later place.

Mat 5:23 Therefore if thou bring thy gift to the altar, and there rememberest that thy brother hath ought against thee;
Mat 5:24 Leave there thy gift before the altar, and go thy way; first be reconciled to thy brother, and then come and offer thy gift.

This man needs to come back to the church whom he lied to, stole their money for an illegitimate defense program and led the people down a path of deception. He needs to go to the boys that he molested and apologize, making any restitution possible in the name of Christ, seeking forgiveness. He needs to ask his wife and old friends for forgiveness for having them lie for him on the witness stand in a U.S. court of law. He needs to apologize to everyone that he's lied to over the years as he's covered his past and deceived them. He needs to repent to the churches that he's lied to over the last few years, including the one who hired him as an associate pastor.

Many good people have told me over the years that they believe he's repented. These people really just want this situation to go away. Because they're not strongly versed in New Testament government and apostolic authority, they try to reason these tough situations away. I strongly oppose their comments with the following:

1. Repentance means to turn around and go the other way. This man has never turned around and gone the other

way. He still hangs around with young boys, he's never apologized or shown remorse for those that he's used, abused and stolen from, and he continues to live in a deceptive lie that he invites others into.

2. This man has never come back to the apostolic governing institution that bound him into Satan's flesh eating agenda and who loosed him from true Holy Spirit inspired active participation in the body of Christ. Typically whoever binds is the one who must loose. Whoever looses is the one who must bind. God is not double minded and He doesn't operate in the confusion of different churches doing different things.

3. Unless a man repents, there is no grace actively available for his salvation. This is the bedrock of our Christian faith. Therefore, if this man is not walking in repentance, he cannot receive grace for salvation and to live a holy and Godly life in Christ Jesus.

4. If a man refuses to walk in repentance and restitution, he clearly doesn't understand the love of God, the gift of Christ on the cross nor the plan of salvation, and he is unqualified to preach, teach or explain the gospel of salvation in any forum. His ministry is invalid.

I've heard all of the honest, sincere, good hearted rebuttals to this form of apostolic New Testament government. They range from the following:

We're not supposed to be mean to people like this!

Jesus would never do something like this!

It's not right that you should judge someone like this!

Judge not, lest you be judged!

God wouldn't want us to ever reject someone!

What you have done is not nice at all!

I don't know why for sure, but I just don't agree with you!

To these thoughts and comments I refer you back to the Word of God. I also remind you that it was red letter, New Testament Jesus who told you to bind and loose with all authority and that He would stand in your midst as the third witness to judge the matter. The New Testament Holy Spirit struck Ananias & Saphira dead for their contemptible living before a pure and holy God. Paul the apostle commanded you to dis-fellowship, don't eat with, don't associate with and mark anyone who's living in overt and willful sin, or who's divisive in nature. Will you obey the New Testament Word of God, or will you persist in disobeying for the sake of your ease and friendship with the world?

(James 4:4) Ye adulterers and adulteresses, know ye not that the friendship of the world is enmity with God? Whosoever therefore will be a friend of the world is the enemy of God.

I close this section with this in mind. The reasons are many for activating the New Testament government of God in this area:

1. It's the highest form of God's love to protect the body of Christ against those who have a form of godliness but whose lifestyles deny His power.
2. It's the highest form of God's love to expose to the offending individual(s) their sin and corruption, issuing a command to repent and be saved from sure destruction and judgment from almighty God. Open shame works in many cases.
3. It's done in the Spirit of restoration, with hope and prayer that the individual will come to his or her senses and repent, making full restitution for the overt sin that has been committed against God, the people of God or the community at large.
4. It's done in extreme humility and with fear and trembling, knowing that prideful judgment in arrogance will reap the same fall from grace as the one who's being judged.

5. It's done with an active plan to restore the individual(s) once they repent, making an honest and sincere effort to make restoration and restitution, and to change their lifestyles.

There is much more to say about this subject but the Holy Spirit and the Word of God will teach you as you have need. I promise you this, this occasion will arise. Be prepared and utilize New Testament Government procedure by the book. God will back you up as you express your highest honor and love for His Word, His government and His commands.

AUTHOR'S NOTE: Two weeks before this book went to print I had what I'd call a miraculous and shocking appointment. I had moved out of the state months before, but was back in town and in our ministry office for only 2 hours one day. During that two hour period, the man in the story above walked in and said that he had been looking for me, though he'd heard that I had moved out of town. He was just as shocked to find me there, as I was that he had found me. He was evidently coming in to get my new address. He had just found me in person.

We had a humbling two hour conversation where this man earnestly apologized and repented for all of his actions and 12 years of silent skirting of the people of the church. He told me that he had no agenda at all except to make things right with those that he'd hurt and offended years ago. We discussed the gravity and weight of this matter and he bore full responsibility. He offered to do whatever was necessary to correct the error and restore all of the people affected. He told of how he was submitted to a ministry and had been getting legitimate help for his former lifestyle. He told of how he used to be a walking time bomb in times past because of his former bondages. He knew that who ever was closest to him when he exploded, that those would be hurt the most. He apologized that our church happened to be that one closest at the time of his destruction.

At the end of this meeting, he agreed to write a letter to the ministry leaders who were involved in the governmental disfellowship process, and I agreed to take it to them with my recommendation. I prayed for him and assured him of our forgiveness and release of his actions in the past. I reminded him that we had personally forgiven him 12 years ago and that we had no bitterness or resentment towards him at all. We parted that day as friends, with communication restored and with his life on the way to towards restoration and healing.

This was one of the greatest days in my life and ministry, to see that a man would come back, even after 12 years of church government action. It was a "Glory to God" moment for myself, my family and our ministry staff! I knew that this return was meant to be included in this book for the sake of encouraging all who must take appropriate action in their churches. To God be the glory!

Paul forgave and received the man who had walked in non-repentant incest, and who later returned in repentance. Once disfellowshipped, this man was now received back into the church with confirmation and love.

(2 Cor 2:6 KJV) Sufficient to such a man is this punishment, which was inflicted of many.
(2 Cor 2:7 KJV) So that contrariwise ye ought rather to forgive him, and comfort him, lest perhaps such a one should be swallowed up with overmuch sorrow.
(2 Cor 2:8 KJV) Wherefore I beseech you that ye would confirm your love toward him.
(2 Cor 2:9 KJV) For to this end also did I write, that I might know the proof of you, whether ye be obedient in all things.
(2 Cor 2:10 KJV) To whom ye forgive any thing, I forgive also: for if I forgave any thing, to whom I forgave it, for your sakes forgave I it in the person of Christ;
(2 Cor 2:11 KJV) Lest Satan should get an advantage of us: for we are not ignorant of his devices.

My prayer is that we see God's governmental actions dealt in love, bringing full circled repentance in the church.

Chapter 7 Review Points

- Make sure your advertising and image display excellence.
- Consider radio and television as powerful mediums to reach people.
- Utilize the most valuable resource – volunteers.
- Handle pastoral confidences correctly.
- Decide if a Christian school is for you.
- Find a good youth leader and empower him.
- Protect your ministry with the right insurance.
- Use the power of networking relationships
- Know how to dis-fellowship a person from the body of Christ
- Make a stand of love against sin in the church.

Chapter 8
Money Help

MINISTRY TITHING

Tithing is one of the bedrock principles in ministry which has to be finalized in your heart early on. It is the foundational principle of the church and the absolute requirement for the blessing of God. If you don't tithe, you will raise up people who don't tithe. If they don't tithe, scripture says that there will be a curse on the whole group of you.

(Mal 3:8 - 12 KJV) Will a man rob God? Yet ye have robbed me. But ye say, Wherein have we robbed thee? In tithes and offerings. Ye are cursed with a curse: for ye have robbed me, even this whole nation. Bring ye all the tithes into the storehouse, that there may be meat in mine house, and prove me now herewith, saith the LORD of hosts, if I will not open you the windows of heaven, and pour you out a blessing, that there shall not be room enough to receive it. And I will rebuke the devourer for your sakes, and he shall not destroy the fruits of your ground; neither shall your vine cast her fruit before the time in the field, saith the LORD of hosts. And all nations shall call you blessed: for ye shall be a delightsome land, saith the LORD of hosts.

Many ministers come up with the craziest stories on why they don't tithe or why they tithe into their own ministries. However, none of these stories are founded on scripture or sound biblical principle. A ministry that hasn't completely surrendered to the principle of tithing will never really get off the ground, and will be constantly hindered, attacked and frustrated by the devil and the curse that they brought upon themselves. I don't know of

ONE church that has ever started with the stand of no tithes that is still in operation a year later. It just can't prosper!

SUCCESS PARABLE:
When you touch the principle of money, you touch God's glory.
If you won't give glory to God, you won't succeed in ministry –
period.

My story starts when I was just getting started with my ministry. I had never been a giver before, and I didn't know just how far I would personally take that tithing – teaching thing. I finally decided that I would tithe because of continued, extreme, personal financial difficulties, and the best place that I could give my tithe was into my own ministry. I went into further terrible financial failure and couldn't figure out why God wasn't helping me out with my money issues. Finally I realized through prayer that I was afraid to let go of that 10%. I had lived in such a poverty mentality all of my life, and I needed that 10% along with the other 90%. Therefore I maintained control of the total 100% by giving it into my own ministry checking account where I could write the check where I needed it to go. This was a deadly mistake as the enemy had full, accursed access to my money, my health, my family and my home, cars and equipment. It was a tragedy in the making.

Through a horrible bankruptcy and attack on my personal family, I finally learned that the way to live by faith and obedience was to get the 10% out of my own hands, out of my control and into the hands of the ministry that was teaching and training me up in the Lord. The ministry that was covering me was worthy of my tithe as Mal. 3:10 said. Once I finally broke free from the fear of losing that 10%, I finally started walking in the blessing of God. The attacks of the enemy totally stopped in my life, family and ministry.

I found my true covering. It was like finding a much needed umbrella in a downpour. The satanic rain just stopped! From that day on, I learned how the Kingdom of God works. I've been on both sides of this principle and I'm here to tell you that the side of obedience and faith in God's plan is the only way to go. Learn from my stripes, wounds and bankruptcy, please!

I talked with a man not long ago who told me that he was going into full time ministry. He said that his pastor had taught him that he needs to tithe into his own ministry. I pray for him because that's the last thing that you can afford to do. Bring the whole tithe into the storehouse. Do you feed and nurture yourself in the Word of God? Do you give yourself all of the revelation and advice in the Word? Do you cover your own self from satanic attack, and do you pray for yourself when you get into trouble and need the power of agreement? If you answered yes to all of these questions, then will you be able to preach your own funeral when your life comes screeching to an early halt? I doubt it. Just obey God and watch the blessings flow because of your willingness to flow with His plan in your life.

THE SECRET OF PERPETUAL SEED MONEY INCREASE

At some time in your ministry, you will receive some seed money from God. It might be from a large offering or from the sale of property that your church doesn't need anymore. We needed some perpetual seed money to raise funds with, and I went before the church. I told them that they had an opportunity to invest into a church program that would continually perpetuate itself over and over again. We were going to enter into a perpetual program that would never put the seed principle at risk. It would always be used to increase. Once I explained this to the people, we quickly raised thousands of dollars and then began investing those funds into creative fund raisers to double that money over and over again. To this date we still have that seed money and we continue to multiply it for ministry programs in need of cash. That offering given by the people has multiplied itself 100 times over and we still have the original seed in our hands!

You can do the same thing. Catching a hold of this principle is liberating for a ministry. It's important that every leader of every church program gets a-hold of this revelation. Each department of your ministry should have perpetual monetary seed in it that can be used to multiply and double itself over and over again. With this seed money in place, all of your department leaders can learn this very powerful principle of multiplication and increase. They can meet together and make their own plans to raise funds for their ministry department without having to constantly tap into the general fund. You've heard the old saying, "It takes money to make money". Here's your opportunity.

Be wise with this seed money. Too many people eat their seed during drought, and then they have nothing to plant or work with when it's time to sow. God is watching what you do with your precious seed, so don't do this. Develop a character that refuses to touch the seed for any other purpose but to multiply it. Demand that it returns into the fund once it's used. Take God's method (Gen. 1:28) and command increase and multiplication with this seed money. Watch over this money and make it work for you like a hired worker.

(To catch this revelation more fully, I recommend that you read one of my favorite financial books, "The Richest Man In Babylon". You can find a link to this book at our web site www.baicsforsuccess.com)

Don't let people touch your seed if they're fools with their own money. Reserve this seed investment money for people and programs that know how to work and multiply seed. Also, don't get into risky "get rich quick" schemes. You may be saying, "What do I do with these funds?". There's a thousand things that you can do with them, and God will begin to open the doors to you and your staff when you seek Him in prayer.

Here's what we did with our investment funds from time to time.

TRUCKLOAD OF POWER WHEELS
We went to a liquidator and purchased an entire semi truckload of the famous Power Wheels trucks, motorcycles and three wheelers which you can buy at your favorite discount store. They were all in their manufacturers boxes but they all had a problem of some kind. They were each missing one part or bolt, or the customer who returned them couldn't get them together properly, or the customer just lied and said that parts were missing in order to get their money back. The retail store sent them back to the Power Wheels company for a refund. Then Power Wheels liquidated them out to us. The truckload price was around $6,000 for 200 of these power wheels. We knew that we could put these power wheels together and sell them for 60% of retail value (assembled and working), and we'd make a wonderful profit with our $6,000.

Our church volunteers got together with screwdrivers and pliers, and we put teams of people on the different models. One crew worked on the Barbie Jeep, the other worked on the Three Wheeler, and the other worked on the G.I. Joe jeeps. After the first couple of units, we got pretty good at assembling them. Each one took around 30 minutes to fully assemble and test out with a fully charged battery.

After three evenings of assembly with our volunteer crew, we rented a U-Haul truck and put the assembled Power Wheels in the back. That Saturday we got permission from store owners and we set up a car lot out in front of different businesses in town. The people almost crashed their cars to get pulled in and to have their children test drive these vehicles. We had three locations on Saturday morning at 10 AM, and by 3pm we were sold out of 200 Power Wheels. The average discounted price of the Power Wheels was $67.50 with some of the nicer ones as high as $159. Doing the math, we sold over $13,500 in Power Wheels in 5 hours and had nothing left. We swept out the U-Haul before returning it and made a healthy youth ministry profit of $7,500 in three nights assembly, one day of sales and a $6,000 seed. The sale took place in June, not at Christmas time.

TAPE AND CD MINISTRY
We got into the Tape and CD ministry by purchasing the needed equipment and blank CD's and tapes. We used our seed money to start this ministry, and before long we were selling the weekly church messages and special ministry series on cassette and CD. We recuperated our initial seed investment and are still selling tapes and CD's to this day. We use the equipment that now makes our ministry a profit, helping to fuel our growing audio/video department.

SPECIAL HELP SERIES PROJECT
We got together in our recording studio and digitally produced a wonderful *"Help In Times Of Trouble"* CD which ministers the powerful Word of God to people who are in desperate need of healing and deliverance. The CD has been responsible for many healing miracles in people's lives as they simply listen to it every day while going to work, at home or in the car. In order to put out this CD we had to have seed money. We invested our seed money into the project and the first sales paid back the seed money. From that point on, the CD has sustained itself and reproduces it's own funds for purchasing more product when the stock gets low.

See this "Help In Times Of Trouble" CD on our web site at www.basicsforsuccesse.com .

KRISPE KREME DONUT FUND RAISER
We purchased a pallet of Krispe Kreme donuts once and stood on the street corners and sold them to passers by. Most people don't like our city's long lines at the Krispe Kreme shop and they saw that they could have a fresh dozen of donuts for the

same price by stopping at our little stand with no wait. We sold the pallet of donuts that day and doubled our money. The donuts cost us $2.50 per dozen as a non-profit organization and we sold them for the Krispe Kreme retail price of $5.00. That was an easy $1,000 profit in three hours of work.

AUTO SALES

We decided to purchase a couple of wholesale cars for our youth ministry once, and we had an auto dealer's wisdom available to help us. We had enough seed money to purchase two cars at $1,500 each. Our youth group washed, waxed and detailed the cars and put them up for sale. One car sold in 4 days and the other sold in two weeks. We made $1,000 per car and the only work we had in them was around 45 minutes each to detail and wash them. That totals $2,000 in 1 ½ hours of work. Not bad for a youth fund raiser!

By the way, we don't do youth car washes anymore. We have seed money! Car wash money is hard money to earn. At the end of a hard working hot day in the sun, the 20 of us made $150 - $200 before we'd take out the cost of soap, food and drinks. We could have worked for $1.50 an hour somewhere and made more money for our youth ministry without the sunburns.

You will find many ways to sow your seed money into fund raising ventures once you have that seed money in your hands. However, DON'T EAT YOUR SEED! Keep it around for generations to come. Imagine the funds that can be raised once every department of your ministry gets their own seed money!

See our section on Creative Fund Raising to get more powerful ideas on how to utilize your seed money and make it double over and over again each year. You can get this information at www.basicsforsuccess.com .

APPROPRIATE SALARIES AND TAX LAWS

This section has such a wide range of margin to it because a true servant of God will certainly follow God's leading in spite of the financial remunerations offered. Knowing this, we will discuss proper salaries and some beneficial tax laws.

(1 Tim 5:17 - 18) Let the elders that rule well be counted worthy of double honour, especially they who labour in the word and doctrine. For the scripture saith, Thou shalt not muzzle the ox that treadeth out the corn. And, The labourer is worthy of his reward.

Every minister who gives his or her life for the Kingdom of God is worthy of double honor and finances. Just as you wouldn't starve the ox that is doing your work and as you wouldn't let your car run out of gas when it's taking you to work, we can't allow a minister of God's Kingdom to starve and go away unfed.

What does it mean to feed the ox? If that ox has treaded out the grain all day, he deserves to eat his fill and be abundantly blessed in his work so he'll be strong and healthy for the next day of work.

What does it mean to give double honor to an elder? In my opinion, that means that you take the average income of the church that they're ministering to – across the board, then double it. This is called "HONOR" and it's worth every penny spent.

As of this writing, it's nothing for the leader of a smaller business corporation to make $150,000 - $300,000 per year plus perks, retirement and other incentives. It should be nothing for the leader of a ministry organization to make the same. A nurse who visits patient's beds daily makes around $40,000 - $60,000 per year. A chaplain can also make $75,000 per year visiting hospital beds for various non-profit organizations. A doctor of medicine will make between $300,000 - $600,000 per year depending on his expertise. A doctor of ministry can also make the same depending on his or her expertise in the field of ministry.

The Business Of Ministry

Now lets be realistic. I know youth pastors who are working in full-time ministry for $100 per week. I also know youth pastors who are working full time for $75,000 per year plus a ministry vehicle, housing allowance, retirement fund and expense account.

I know pastors who work separate jobs in order to bless their church finances, and they may get a token salary of some kind each month. I know other pastors who make $24,000 per year, and still others who make $200,000 per year. I find that each pastor and each church is set up differently with different salary structures and benefits. You will find that many salary levels are based on the poverty or prosperity spirit in which the people of the church walk in.

If you show me a church full of millionaires, I'll show you a church that will not allow their pastor to work a second job to make his living. They'll bless his family greatly and make sure that he's honored according to the general lifestyle of that church.

Show me a church of welfare based, poverty stricken people and I'll show you a church that's going to have to pray in a sacrificial and tenacious pastor who is willing to sow into them and the vision while he also works outside of the church.

I recommend that you get on the internet and find the sites that will give you a general overview of what people are getting paid in your area. You can type in the field of work and your zip code and these sites will give you the high and low salaries and the general median income for that type of work. These sites will include salaries for ministers, leaders of non-profit organizations, chaplains, pastors, etc. You might be shocked to see what many ministers in your area are receiving as paychecks.

Don't feel bad about believing God for a $200,000 per year income. Ministry is your life. You could take your creative gifts and make millions in the real world but you've constrained

167

yourself to His calling and service. You're like the Old Testament Levites who have no other inheritance but the Lord. Therefore, you've got to provide for the needs of your family, lay up an inheritance and save for a so-called retirement plan. You've got to be a good man and leave enough of an inheritance that will bless your grandchildren, and you've got to get your kids through school and be a blessing to your wife, community, church and spiritual father. You'll also need to care for your natural parents in their old age. Beloved, you're not going to do that successfully on $24,000 annually for the rest of your life.

Silence the voices in your head and all around you that would condemn you for prospering in God's ministry. Jesus was very wealthy in His ministry, the Levite priests lived very well under God's blessing, and you should prosper and live well too.

I'm not telling you that there won't be a time in your life that you need to sow your services into a church that can't afford you. I'm confident that you'll have to give, sow and multiply yourself by faith at times when the finances are not there for you to receive. However, when your increase and reward begins to come, don't feel bad or condemned about receiving it as your inheritance! God wants to bless you financially for performing His Kingdom duties that many others refused to perform when they said "no".

TAX LAWS

There are some very beneficial and powerful tax laws that a licensed or ordained minister can benefit from which are worth noting. I am not claiming to be a tax specialist or an attorney and am only telling you my opinion. You will need to get your own professional help when preparing to make tax preparations of your own.

F.I.C.A. TAX EXEMPTION
(U.S. Ministries)

As a licensed or ordained minister, you have the distinct option of exempting yourself from the social security tax plan that takes a large percentage of everyone's paycheck. As a religious decision you can fill out an IRS form that will allow you to disqualify yourself from the current social security plan. This will allow you to keep all social security taxes that would otherwise be taken out of your salary.

There are consequences to this move, some of which include:

1. You have to determine if you think that social security will even be around when you get to retirement age.

2. If you keep social security, you have to determine if you are willing to live on the small sum that it gives you (poverty income level) without going back to work to gain extra money. If you become re-employed, your social security check gets smaller.

3. You can only deduct ministry income from this opt-out plan. In other words, if you make a ministry income and also have another business or job that makes you money, you will be required to pay F.I.C.A. taxes on that non-ministry income even after signing a withdrawal form.

4. Once you sign the withdrawal form, depending on IRS sentiment at the time, you may be allowed to enter back into the system once only. However if you enter back into the system you will never be able to withdrawal again at a later date.

5. If you save 7 – 15% of your income from being taken by F.I.C.A., do you have a plan set in motion that will invest this money for a long term retirement program of your own, or are you simply going to lose this money by eating your seed year after year – assimilating the extra into your daily income needs? This would be devastating when you need a supplemental retirement income and find that there's not anything in the account and no social security plan for you to tap into.

169

PARSONAGE ALLOWANCE
(U.S. Ministries)

As of the writing of this book there is still one of the greatest tax deductions available to ministers called the parsonage allowance. This is one of the last remaining double deductions on the tax law books and it's available to you if you're a paid and licensed/ordained minister.

The church board or corporate board that employs you can assign a portion of your annual income as a parsonage allowance. *This must be done by the church or organization board having a board of directors meeting at the beginning of the year, and setting a designated amount as a parsonage allowance, equal to the amount you think that you will be spending for the year. Make sure that you plan your house repairs and furniture updates in advance so you can include them in the parsonage allowance costs.* If you own or rent a home that costs you $1,000 per month in payments, plus another $200 per month to keep it up, pay the lawn mowing service, keep the pool full of water, keep the shingles nailed down, etc... then you have a $14,400 parsonage allowance. If you had to purchase a refrigerator or any furnishings for that parsonage, this also ads to the value of the parsonage allowance. Say that you had to purchase $4,000 in appliances and furniture during this year and your parsonage allowance is now up to $18,400 in expenses. As long as the church board records an authorized parsonage allowance of $18,400 on their meeting minutes at the beginning of the year, then at the end of the year, you get to take that parsonage allowance directly off of line 1 of your 1040 return. In other words, if you were paid $36,000 for the year in salary but your parsonage allowance was $18,400, then the taxable income amount that you will start with on line 1 of the 1040 is only $17,600. From there you will begin to include all of your standard deductions if you fill out the long form. That's where your house interest will become a double deduction. You will get to include all of the interest paid on your house loan, after you already deducted the full house payment off of the top of your income. This is a real blessing and if used correctly, it's benefit can actually pay for your house in the long run. Remember that your parsonage allowance, though it is deductible from line 1 of your 1040, is still subject to the full F.I.C.A. tax unless you have opted out of the social security plan.

It's important to get a good tax consultant who is familiar with ministry parsonage allowances. I've had good ones and I've had bad ones that I had to teach this law to. Search around and find the one that all of the other ministers are using.

BUSINESS EXPENSES

Remember that there are certain ministry expenses that you can use as tax write off's including association dues, conference fees, travel mileage and ministry meals where you are performing your ministry duties while at a restaurant. However, remember that the IRS will only allow you to write off 50% of your ministry meals as a deduction *(as of this writing)*. Therefore you might want to make an arrangement with your church where the ministry pays for all ministry meals where you have to counsel or communicate at a restaurant. That way there is no need to use deductions in this area and you don't lose 50% of your deduction through this new law.

There are many more deductions, tips and secrets that a good tax preparer can help you with. I encourage you to seek out a good one and run these pages by him or her to make sure that current IRS tax code still applies.

HOW TO SAVE 50% ON ALL ITEMS THAT YOU PURCHASE

There is a way that you can get twice as much done in your church with the money you spend, get twice as many books and study materials, and empower your sheep with more materials than before imagined.

Start a bookstore in your church. In the days of Christian bookstore transitions, acquisitions, failures, takeovers, etc., the way of the future is a "Local Church Bookstore". You represent all of the consumer buyers of your church. They come to your place of ministry every week. They listen to your advice on which books to read and they gladly eat whatever you point them to. You are already in every sense of the word, a Christian bookstore just waiting to happen. Christian bookstores survive on 42 – 50% markup of all books, music, gifts and supplies. If you are an official bookstore, you too can experience the joy of getting 50% off of your purchases. I highly recommend that you set up a corner, a room or place in your foyer where people will see your bookstore. Sell the books and supplies for retail or slightly below. Your people will gladly pay this price for the product, and this will create funds for your bookstore to grow, for you to buy additional products to give away, or to support a great missionary. You can supply the people with teachers and student manuals for Sunday school, new bibles, bible software, great new music CD's and DVD's, Christian T-shirts and apparel, and the greatest books and bibles of all time for Christians to purchase and read. These things can come from your bookstore. What a great service to provide to your people!

How do I start a bookstore? It's easy. Your church may be XYZ Ministries and your bookstore will be called XYZ Bookstore. When someone writes a check to your XYZ Bookstore, it is simply deposited into your XYZ Church account.

How do I get product for my bookstore? It's easy. Contact various suppliers and let them know that you are a bookstore and you are requesting wholesale pricing. Make it clear that you are a wholesaler and will be retailing the merchandise to your customers. These wholesalers will gladly sell to you at deeply discounted prices. They will send you catalogs, tell you the best selling items and will help you select what you need for your bookstore. You might have a minimum quantity that you have to buy, but be prepared to meet the minimum. You'll sell the items if you order the items that your people need and want. We have valuable links to bookstore items that you may want to carry at your bookstore at www.basicsforsuccess.com .

The internet is a great place to find suppliers of the products that you want. Remember, if it's sitting on a retail store shelf, there's a supplier or manufacturer somewhere behind the scenes who will also sell it to you at a deep discount. This is called wholesale and retail business. You can save thousands of dollars per year by stepping into this reality.

There is an association that Christian bookstores can join called CHRISTIAN BOOKSELLERS ASSOCIATION (C.B.A.). Look them up on the internet. They have an annual convention that you should consider attending whether you're a member or not. It will cost you a little money to attend, but it will be money well spent. You will meet the top authors and music artists in Christianity and get free personally autographed books from them. You will meet everyone in the Christian bookstore industry, go to free Christian concerts and training sessions, and you will be loaded down with catalogs and free samples from hundreds of Christian bookstore suppliers and manufacturers. These 4 days in my opinion are one of the best eye-opening, life-changing experiences for a ministry. The wisdom that you gain and the contacts that you make during that conference will be invaluable for your ministry. The conference is held in the middle of the year at a different city each year.

With all that said, you should start saving 50% immediately and start providing a vital service of servant-hood to the people involved in your ministry. This is the way of the future for all churches so don't miss the cutting edge of supporting your people with the items they need, and enjoying 50% off of everything that you buy for your ministry.

KEEPING YOUR HANDS PUBLICLY
CLEAN AROUND MONEY

Make sure that you set protective measures for yourself and your workers concerning the finances. Don't allow the accuser an open door to harm your volunteers or staff, or to discredit your good character.

1. Never allow less than two qualified people to receive, count and record the offerings. Make sure that they count and double count the money. They need to keep all envelopes and notes as to where the money is designated to. They need to have a record sheet where they both sign off with signatures on the offering amounts. It's not impossible, but it's harder for two people to come into agreement to steal church offerings. Therefore, switch those who count the offerings on a normal basis. Have 4 – 6 people designated and put them on a weekly rotation. Make this a policy in your ministry for the protection of your people. There's nothing worse than giving your life as a volunteer into a ministry only to have some devil point his finger at you and accuse you of dipping into the funds. This policy will stop that accusation cold and will protect your volunteers, elders and staff.

2. Make sure that there is a cross check done between the first round counters, the treasurer and the actual deposit made into the church account. Have people sign off with signatures on an official form to show that the deposit was made by someone other than the initial counters of the offerings. Also, have the person who makes the deposit sign the deposit receipt, circling and verifying the amount deposited, and the deposit receipt is given to the treasurer or bookkeeper for verification.

3. Have all checks and payments supported with a valid receipt or acquisition request form filled out. Require that your staff bring receipts for funds used as a part of policy. This is a protective measure in place to help them, not as a point of mistrust. The mistrust stands

174

with the accuser of the brethren, and the policies are in place to protect the staff who handles the money.

4. Wherever there are financial transactions taking place, make sure that your policies include double handling of the funds.

A QUALIFIED TREASURER

The treasury is one of the most important elements of your ministry. It's in the treasury that God watches to see what ethics you operate under. He watches the handling of the money, how it is divided up and what levels of honor are given through the treasury. Money represents people's lives. They have given a portion of precious life to receive their money, and then they gave that money into the treasury. This money represents *"life"*.

The most important area of the treasury "in my opinion" is a good watchman and keeper of the treasury. It's vital that the person(s) who watch over the finances be above reproach, without a bad credit history, ones who are not late with their personal bills and ones who have a proper attitude about money, God's money, and strong faith to handle God's business. This is a tall order. There aren't a lot of people that can handle this *"most important"* area of your ministry.

For the position of treasurer, you need to find that right person who has an anointing to handle money. The Old Testament shows that faithful men were to be in charge of the treasuries. The treasury and spiritual appropriation of funds and perfumes was the downfall of Judas who was Jesus' treasurer. I Timothy gives clear detail that overseers *(treasurers)* must be men of noble character and tempered.

(1 Tim 3:2 KJV) A bishop then must be blameless, the husband of one wife, vigilant, sober, of good behaviour, given to hospitality, apt to teach;

175

The Business Of Ministry

(1 Tim 3:3 KJV) Not given to wine, no striker, not greedy of filthy lucre; but patient, not a brawler, not covetous;
(1 Tim 3:4 KJV) One that ruleth well his own house, having his children in subjection with all gravity;
(1 Tim 3:5 KJV) (For if a man know not how to rule his own house, how shall he take care of the church of God?)
(1 Tim 3:6 KJV) Not a novice, lest being lifted up with pride he fall into the condemnation of the devil.
(1 Tim 3:7 KJV) Moreover he must have a good report of them which are without; lest he fall into reproach and the snare of the devil.

I personally look for someone that I could trust with my life. I want someone who has great faith in God and His ability to provide. I need someone who speaks faith over our ministry's finances instead of doubt and unbelief. I want them looking for the answer to the problem instead of complaining that there's not enough in the account. I need a Joshua and Caleb spirit that says "We can surely possess the land", instead of a calculating, negative, spy-spirit who says, "We'd better cut back and save because tough times are ahead of us and God can't come through with His promises". I need a person who's a real giver, and who doesn't have a problem giving by faith and giving ministry finances as seed-faith offerings when times are tough. This person must believe in the seed-time and harvest principle and must be firmly rooted and grounded in personal tithing and giving of seed-faith offerings.

Jesus had a treasurer to take care of his vast funding of ministry. Unfortunately this treasurer couldn't handle the responsibilities of His ministry, and was always questioning His actions with the money and why He allowed a woman to pour expensive perfume to anoint Him. This frustration with Jesus' faith and direction of the funds ended up cutting into his own faith in the Son of God. He ended up determining that this Jesus must not be the messiah. In his opinion, Jesus didn't have the capacity, wisdom or faith to bring God's Kingdom on earth *(as Judas thought it would happen through revolt).* He lost faith because of the finances,

176

and he ended up selling out on Jesus for 30 pieces of silver. Note that the sell out and betrayal of Jesus included money, which became Judas' weakness because he was not strong enough to handle the Kingdom treasury. This should be a very powerful lesson and word picture for us today. Your treasurer is no less open to this sort of attack and failure in his/her life. Don't be ignorant of these principles

Once you have chosen your qualified treasurer, make sure that you develop policies to cover and protect this person with all the strength and wisdom that you have. Also, double check all entries and accounts on a weekly or monthly basis. Pray for your treasurer. Sit down frequently with your treasurer and pull out the church bills. Both of you agree together in faith concerning Matt. 18:19 and agree together that the church account will be able pay all bills on time. If there's a bill that's late, don't frequently allow your church treasurer to take those hits of having to explain *"why"* the bill is constantly late. This is your ministry. You must get involved in the phone calls and explaining to those that you're delinquent with. This protection is a must for the spiritual and mental health of the treasurer. Remember, they're keeping and watching the treasury for you, but they are not the one in final authority over the treasury. You are. Therefore, don't give up your responsibility with the finances but take up your authority and protect your treasurer's heart and soul.

It's important to frequently reward your treasurer for doing the books and keeping track of everything. Praise them openly at least once per year in front of the church for the hard work that they've done. Have the people pray for them and bless them. Take your treasurer out for a lunch or dinner and thank them for a job well done.

I know a minister who had a treasurer doing all of his work for him. He was a missionary and was bringing in $7,000 - $12,000 per month into the ministry account. He had many donors at $15 - $50 per month, and a few larger givers. He had general accounts, building funds, children's feeding funds and other accounts that this poor treasurer/accountant had to handle. She worked tirelessly into the night hours as a volunteer to make sure that the funds were accounted for correctly and deposited on time so this man could withdraw the funds on the other side of the world quickly. This girl was loyal, faithful and a strong promoter of his ministry. However, on one of his annual trips back to the states, this man reamed this lady for misplacing $2.50 over the year. She had successfully accounted for $100,000 + with a thousand of transactions over that year. Over the course of that year, she misplaced and could not account for $2.50. This man came to town and in his first meeting and comments to her, made it known that under no uncertain terms, he was not pleased with her loss of that $2.50, and that she should make up the funds that were lost from her own pocket. Needless to say, she began backing away, stopped supporting him personally and she ended her giving of her time and heart into his ministry. It was simply because her great gift and watchful eye over his ministry went unnoticed and unappreciated. She felt as if he was using her, and indeed her feelings were justified. I watched this happen from a first hand point of view. Incidentally, this wonderful treasurer is now my treasurer, and I'll personally pay the $2.50 in misplaced funds if this ever happens to me because I appreciate her immensely!

Pastors and ministers, please bless your treasurer! They're worthy of their weight in gold!

GRANTS, GRANT WRITERS, THE PROCESS:

One of the powerful ways that non-profit organizations receive money to operate their programs is through grant funding. There are many corporations, individuals and government groups that offer funding for certain types of projects and programs. However, this grant process is generally tedious and requires patience, newly developed skill and a learning curve that many Christians are not willing to participate in.

Many Christians *(including ministers)* have a mindset that looks to God to supply all of their needs without their co-operation and joint partnership. However, I have come to find through my years of ministry that God develops leaders who will move "with" Him in joint partnership. We make a move, then He moves, then we move again, and then He moves again. It's kind of like a dance or a chess game with both players moving towards the same goal together.

Grant funding is available for ministries such as yours but you must work hard, research and begin to learn this new field of finance. There are areas that you will have to comply with if you want to receive these funds. You will also need to learn to use the world's buzz words and mind set when writing a grant request. You will have to depart from your Christian lingo when it comes to grant writing. That's enough in itself to drive many lazy Christians out of the grant writing field. You have to realize that a business or corporation generally isn't interested in giving funds to a ministry organization that, "Blesses the sanctified saints with the powerful enrichment of God's Holy Word." They will however give into a community development program that *"Educates the community's adults or youth in motivational life and family skills"*. Same activity – two ways of saying it.

Corporate Grants:

There are plenty of corporations in your area that offer thousands or millions of dollars per year to organizations just like yours. They're attempting to accomplish some specific goals with their money. If you're doing what they want to accomplish, then you have a potential of being funded. Each grant funding corporation will have a defined set of requirements, priorities and goals that you need to read through before considering a grant application, including:

  1. Some will not give to religious organizations.

2. Some will not give to groups that are not 501(c)(3) Organizations.
3. Some will not give to those who don't have audited financial statements.
4. Some will not give into building or capital programs.
5. Some will not give into general operating expenses.
6. Some will not give salary funding.
7. Some want to give into "matching grant" funds, where their dollar is matched elsewhere and doubled in value.

Before wasting any time on writing a tedious grant application, check out what each corporation requires and whether or not you fit within their giving range. Find the best fits for your programs and focus on grant writing with these organizations.

Many Christian ministries began the search for groups that will fund their programs, only to find out that there is no one who is interested in funding them. Sometimes a grant application process is good for us because it will open our own eyes to help us see if we're being effective in our world and if we're actually meeting needs in the highest demand areas. It's an eye opening experience to find out that most groups are not interested in funding our "bless me" clubs and internal ministries. They are going after the hardcore problematic fields of need including homelessness, drug rehabilitation, hunger, career training, life saving education and disaster relief. Many church groups have found it hard to get their tea parties and Bible clubs funded by outside organizations, and those are great wake-up calls for the church to get more involved in the actual needs of the community. We are called to be SALT and LIGHT in a darkened and bland tasting world.

(Mat 5:13 KJV) Ye are the salt of the earth: but if the salt have lost his savour, wherewith shall it be salted? It is thenceforth good for nothing, but to be cast out, and to be trodden under foot of men.
(Mat 5:14 KJV) Ye are the light of the world. A city that is set on an hill cannot be hid.

If we're not salt in this earth then we're of no earthly value and will only be trampled on by men. It's important that our churches, ministries and visions include helping this world from it's curse of poverty, disease, death and shame.

Many corporations won't give into groups that are actively "pickled" in Christianese vocabulary. They don't want to be associated with a church group in specific. They don't want some complaining customer coming to their door to argue doctrine, beliefs, your church history or problems, etc. Therefore you have to make a decision. Either you stay away from these corporations and narrow your field of funding tremendously, or help these corporations to feel comfortable with you, help them to insulate themselves from a complaining public, and serve their purposes while they'll be serving yours *(kind of like your dance with God mentioned above)*. In other words, you might need to change your program name from *"Help Jesus To Feed Jehovah's Hungry Children"* to *"Feed The Children"*. You will need to rid your application of verbal Christianese and heavenly hype. There is no room for speaking of faith in a grant application. Corporations don't have faith and they don't move in faith-filled outcome with those that they give to. They want proven results, not *"hope"* that you will be able to do what you *"believe"* you can do. Many Christian organizations are tempted to say, *"We believe that with these funds we will be able to reach a significant portion of our city with the good news of the gospel, as well as feeding thousands of their most hungry children."* You might rather say, "Based upon the graph that we've provided below, our volunteer teams will be able to reach 416 homes in the first 6 months, and 512 homes in the following 6 months, providing "at risk" families with much needed emergency food supplies."

Grant makers are not interested in faith based statements. The only faith that they are going to operate in is the faith that they've made a good decision based upon your FACTUAL grant request. Unfortunately, facts are something that many churches have a hard time with for the most part because of hyper-faith,

181

heavenly-minded lifestyles. I believe this problem is greatly because many are struggling with failing ministry systems that represent the old wineskin. Many don't want to face the fact that their old, broken down church models aren't working anymore in this present world we live in. *(Our web site has pertinent information on old and new wineskin ministries and how to renew an old one. www.basicsforsuccess.com .*

Generally speaking, corporations don't want to fund a supposed extremist radical group such as *"The First Christian Church of Jesus Christ – Save The Word From Going To Hell Project."* They also don't want to hear you say that you *"believe"* you can reach thousands this year with your program. They're not interested in our hopeful, evangelistic faith campaigns. They don't want to fund the internal workings of a church with the possible thought that their funds might go to purchase your new church pews. They don't want to give into our old-school methods of constructing buildings that will only be used one day per week. They're not into failing business models, and they sure don't want to invest in someone else's 200 year old, antiquated model.

Corporations do want to fund the actual feeding, clothing, educating, rehabilitating and housing of homeless children, *"at risk"* teens and adults. They want to see impoverished families come up out of their dilemma and receive instruction, education, schooling and career training to get them out of poverty guidelines. They want to see crime rates drop, teens staying in school until graduation day, teen pregnancy percentages drop, and inner-city gangs dismembered. They are looking for real answers to today's real problems. I believe that the real church has these answers, but unless the real church is willing and ready to step out onto our streets and become salt again, I don't imagine that there's any grant funds available.

I recommend that you get on the internet and do a thorough search of corporations that give grants. Take an entire day and find out what they are giving into as well as their requirements.

Take notes and find an area of giving that hits close to your heart. Begin to strategize how you could meet these needs effectively with their grant funding, then make plans to write a grant request. Don't take the easy way out and write to Microsoft's Bill Gates. Everyone's already done that and Microsoft is not going to fund you unless you're a cut above all the others. Remember, there's no easy way out in grant writing. It's hard work, requires a lot of research and tenacity, then it requires skilled writers who can put on paper what your organization is doing, in a way that the grant corporation wants to hear it. It will require a learning curve and some time. It's like investing and sowing seed, but it will pay off if you continue steadfast with your vision of helping the needs of your community and world.

Here's a beginning web site listing of information for you to view:
1. www.guidestar.org
2. www.youthdevelopment.org

We have new and updated information available on our web site as well. Go to www.basicsforsuccess.com for more information on this subject.

HIRING A GRANT WRITER

When you enter the wonderful world of grant writing, you are going to be approached by grant writers who are going to convince the novice that it's easy to get a grant. By hiring them you are just a short time away from your first big fat check. Remember that you are probably going to need a grant writer on your team, and at some point you will need to hire an outside person unless you have a highly skilled, highly motivated and a highly creative person who can learn at exponential rate and has the tenacity not to quit in mid-stream of your grant writing program.

Grant writers can be like car salesmen. They're selling you their services. Many can act like they really care about you and your organization. They can act like you have the most wonderful program that is sure to be funded. However, the key word is *"ACT"*. Don't buy the act from just any potential grant writer that comes along. They all get paid to write grant requests. However, they are going to want payment whether or not you get your grant request funded. That means that you pay big dollars, they write you a grant request and they're gone. Did you get funded? Maybe you did, maybe you didn't.

I recommend that you screen your grant writers very closely. Find out what grants they've successfully gotten for other organizations and for how much? Find out if they've secured funding for groups such as yours. Find out if they're versed in working with non-profit church organizations. Find out when their last successful grant was secured. Then shop around and find out how much other grant writers charge. See if they're in the ballpark with their pricing structures.

The ideal setup is to have a grant writer who won't charge you up front for the grant application process. They will be on staff with you and will be paid once your grant request has been successfully funded. There are grant writers who will accept payment in this manner but you will have to search for them. They typically are very good at what they do, they have all of the right contacts and they will honestly believe in your program enough to invest their time and life into writing your grant request.

You might not be able to pay them with actual grant funding dollars, but you can work around that. If your grant funding included your personal salary, then take the salary that you're already making from another source and pay the grant writer from that. There are many ways to find the funds for your grant writer without drawing them from the actual grant funds.

Remember that most grant writers are a dime a dozen. However, you are looking for the one who offers guarantees. No one can absolutely guarantee success with grant writing. However, a grant writer who is willing to invest his or her time and talent up front into your program really believes in what you are doing and believes that it's fundable. These writers are your best option.

FEDERAL AND STATE FUNDING

This is an entirely different monster. Federal and state funds have become more readily available since the faith-based initiative that was instigated by President George Bush. This initiative forces governmental agencies to look at funding faith-based organizations that are doing the grass roots level work. The fact is that much of the benevolence work in America is being done today by the church, but almost all funding is going to non-Christian groups that are not doing the work as successfully as faith-based grass roots groups.

You have a right to these funds if you are doing the work that these funds are provided for. However, it's important to realize that you can't bend federal or state funding to fit your program. You must bend to fit their program. If you are feeding the homeless under the XYZ bridge and the federal grant says that they'll fund the feeding of the homeless under the ABC bridge, then you'd better either move your feeding operation or plan to "not" get funded by the federal government.

Here is an excellent listing of many federal grants that are available each year. I recommend that you take a couple of hours and scan these grants, who qualifies to apply, and exactly what the grant allows for. Mark down the ones that you are really interested in, or that you currently qualify for with your active programs.

www.federalgovernmentgrants.org

Once you find a grant that you believe you could qualify for, then it's imperative to get professional counsel on how to write this grant request. The White House should have a department that teaches grant writing classes around the country. Other non-profit groups are actually funded by government grants to travel around the country and help teach non-profit organizations the "how to" of grant writing for these federal funds.

Some grants are available only to schools. Some are available to the states, who then in turn will hand them out to local grass-roots organizations as they see fit. Some are open to only medical facilities. However, most of them are open to non-profit, charitable organizations just like yours.

Writing a federal grant request can be tedious and time consuming. You literally need to plan on two solid months of work on writing a successful federal grant request if you've never done one before. However, there is some help available.

I've run across different organizations over the years who are masters of helping faith-based organizations to write and receive federal grant funding. They travel the country offering *(sometimes free)* faith-based seminars, grant writing education training sessions, and giving out tremendous instruction and data to anyone who signs up for the class. Search the internet or our web site for these organizations. I recommend that you go to one of their seminars and get educated, and then let them help and guide you through your first federal grant application process.

Concerning state funding, search the internet and ask your congressman, mayor's office, governor or senator for grant funding opportunities. Some of them have mailing lists that you can get onto which tell when new grant opportunities come available. Get on all of those mail and e-mail lists.

There are a few things that any corporation, state or federal grant review board is going to want to see. These are imperatives, and if you can't fulfill these areas to convince the most critical skeptic, then don't waste your time with grant applications.

1. A powerful and meaningful program name.
2. A powerful 25 word statement that clarifies the entire project plan into these 25 words.
3. An emotionally moving 2 page executive summary *(needs statement)* that is filled with undeniable facts, powerful, polled percentages, and a realistic overview of how your program will absolutely answer the need.
4. A convincing project narrative that leaves no stone unturned, tells the whole story and answers all questions possible.
5. You must clearly tell what population will be served by your program.
6. Give the absolute project goals and be specific. Don't use faith based hopes, but explain in detail the absolute goals and priorities of the program over a given period of time.
7. List the program activities and project design for your grant request.
8. Fully list your personnel and their responsibilities. You will need to convince the critics that each person is qualified and has a history in this field that suits what they are about to fund. You will need to include a resume on each person involved, as these grant funds will be actually hiring your people to do the work promised in this grant request.
9. You will need to draw up a timeline graph that shows clearly when the project starts, when the funding is needed, when the funds will be spent, and when the program will end.
10. You will need to explain in detail who will be responsible for managing this grant program and who is responsible for the actual delegation of funds *(with resume)*.
11. You will need to show how this grant will build capacity within your organization. This simply means that you

will show how a grant will help your organization to become stronger and better at what you're doing. You will ramp up to greater ability because of this grant.

12. Very importantly, you must give a defined program of evaluation, to show exactly and specifically how you will be able to measure your actual results at the end of the program. This is very important and critical to grant funding. If you can't measure your success then you are not worthy to be funded once...let alone twice. Find a bullet proof way to analyze and evaluate your program effectiveness.

With federal grant funding, it is important to know that there is currently a so called *"separation of church and state"* when utilizing these funds. You will have to make an ethical decision as to whether or not federal grant funding will work for you. There are government officials that are requesting that non-profit organizations challenge and stretch these boundaries, but unless you're a ground breaking organization that is in for a fight all the way to the Supreme Court, you'd be better off just figuring if you can work within these guidelines.

Scenario #1. You need grant funding so you can preach the gospel to the homeless and to feed them. You've found a grant opportunity that will fund that. However, the government is not at all interested in helping you preach the gospel. They will however, help you feed the homeless. Therefore while you are feeding the homeless on federal grant dollars, you cannot preach the gospel. You can only feed the homeless.

Your grant request asks for the staffing of a soup kitchen downtown from 8am – 1pm each day. You are asking that the grant pays the rent on the building so you can perform these duties. You are going to feed 150 people each day, and you will need X amount of food supplies, equipment and staff to do this. If this grant is funded by the federal government, your hired staff will not be able to preach the gospel in that building during the hours of 8am – 1pm while they're on federal salaried funds.

While the people are coming through the soup line, you can't preach to them. You can only meet the needs that you stated in the federal grant request. However, if someone wants to start up a conversation with you and asks you a spiritual question, you are certainly allowed to give your personal opinion. And what's also great about this program is that after 1pm, the building and equipment (under your care) can be used for any purpose that you deem fit. You can have church in the building, preach the gospel all night long and use the pots and pans as drums if you desire. Just remember that you are under federal government requirements during the timeline that you state in your grant request.

Scenario #2. You want to purchase a semi-truck and trailer that turns into a portable theatre. You're going to go from school to school and pack this high tech theatre with students from the schools that you go to. You're going to teach on abstinence, anti-drug, anti-violence education. The federal and state government is buying or leasing this truck and trailer for your program, as well as the staff to drive it, the gas to fuel it and the maintenance, the training materials and other equipment, promotional materials, mailers, hotels and food. Therefore, you can't preach the gospel during the times of 8am – 3pm when you stated to them that you are doing these seminars at schools. However, you can set that trailer up anywhere you choose after hours and preach the gospel all night long if you choose, as long as you're not on federal government salary and on federal government time.

Scenario #3. You want to provide daycare in your church building for "at risk" families who desperately need childcare in order to fulfill their job requirements. You want the federal government to pay for a portion of your church building payment and you want to be open from 7am – 6pm Monday through Friday. You're going to use one section of your building for this program, and you've figured square footage times hours used into the actual building costs. If you are funded, you and your staff cannot preach the gospel to these children during the child

189

care times that the government is paying you for. They are not interested in funding your gospel, but they are interested in funding the actual care of the children. In all actuality, you've entered into a binding contract with the government and if you break your end of the contract, the federal government can nullify any future payments and require that you repay them for funding already given to you.

You can preach the gospel to these children at any time other than the contracted time that the government is paying for.

If you have a program that can fit into these pre-qualifications, then you should proceed with federal funding requests until you are funded. If you can't do this with a good conscience, then go after other funding sources and forget federal/state funding.

All of these issues will be thoroughly covered by your first conference given by one of the many federal funding educational organizations. Ask questions and make sure that these rules still apply to you and your organization.

WEALTH OF THE WICKED – HOW TO TAP IT

In this day and age, you need to know how to position yourself and your ministry to actively receive the wealth of the wicked. The church in general is totally out of position to receive the world's wealth. We came to Christ destitute, poor, broke and troubled, and He delivered us. Years later, the church is still destitute, poor, broke and troubled with no wealth to speak of. This is not right! We must get into position if we will ever receive the wealth of the wicked.

I don't intend to take up a lot of space in this book to teach on this topic. I have a book on this subject called *"Wealth Transfer, From The Wicked To The Righteous"* . You can find it at our resource center on the web at www.basicsforsuccess.com .

CREATIVE FUNDRAISING IDEAS

Another topic that I have a lot of information in is on fundraising. I actually have so much information on this topic that I wrote a complete booklet on it. You can find this at our resource center on the web. It's called *"Creative Fund Raising 101"* which does an eclipse on the old-school forms of fundraising. Remember, I have 20 years of experience in the ministry and in fundraising. This book is the book I was always looking for as a pastor. Everyone knows how to have a carwash. Are you ready for some new and exciting ways to raise funds? In *"Creative Fund Raising 101"*, you will find many new and exciting ways of fundraising that will help you to get *"out of the box"* with your fundraising.

Chapter 8 Review Points

- Make sure your ministry is a tithing one.
- Use your seed for perpetual increase.
- Choose various fund raisers to involve your ministry with.
- Evaluate and review current ministry salaries and perks.
- Decide whether to opt out of F.I.C.A. tax exemption.
- Learn about and utilize the wonderful tax deduction called "Parsonage Allowance".
- Learn how to maximize your ministry business expenses.
- Start saving 50% on everything your ministry purchases.

191

- Get and keep a qualified treasurer.
- Keep your own hands out of the money.
- Decide if grants should be part of your ministry work.
- Hire the right grant writer.
- Determine whether federal and/or state funding is for you.
- Learn how to tap into the wealth of the wicked.
- Learn how to utilize creative fund raising.
- Visit our web site for more valuable information and free tools.

- The End

www.basicsforsuccess.com

WELCOME TO OUR WEB SITE:

Our ministry team is proud to offer www.basicsforsuccess.com to help you make your next shift or transition effectively and seamlessly. Leaders are taken from glory to glory, step by step in their leadership journeys. www.basicsforsuccess.com is here to serve you during your season of transition.

Leaders are shifting their pastoral based churches to apostolic 5 fold ministry teams. Youth pastors are transitioning to senior pastors. Traveling evangelists are being called home to minister in a local church. Still others are being called to the harvest fields of the world. Old wineskins are being made new. Some leaders are simply leaving the old wineskin and stepping into the new. All of us are being challenged to buy the new field with the great treasure, though it costs all we have. www.basicsforsuccess.com will help you with valuable resources and networking to make your transition less painful and to give you strength and encouragement.

We are continually expanding the resources that are available to you, with a heart to serve you during your time of ministry shift. Please check out the site periodically as the site changes frequently

Please come to www.basicsforsuccess.com and sign up for my free E-News letter as well as many other free ministry tools that we have to offer!

God bless you!
- Dr. Daniel Daves

Children's Feeding Network
www.childrensfeedingnetwork.org

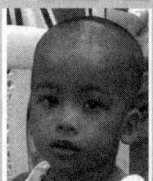

We found 5 year old Maria dying of AIDS in a South African orphanage. Her little 20 lb. despondant body had

Dr. Daniel Daves & Maria

wasted away. Thanks to our nutritional immune building program, she gained weight, strength and health and went back to school. Maria was given a new opportunity to live again! Please give now!

Timely Messages On CD
By Dr. Daniel Daves

THREE KEYS TO YOUR NEXT DIMENSION

When it's time to move up to your next level, there are three imperative keys that will thrust you into your destiny. Without these keys, a person will only become frustrated and confused. **$6.00**

HOW TO CAUSE EARTHLY THINGS TO MOVE WHEN YOU SPEAK *When it's time to*

get a mountain out of your life, you need to learn the keys to speaking and causing earth to move. This message will arm you for movement. **$6.00**

HOW TO LEND AND NOT BORROW

God is demanding that Christians get out of debt, and make the cut from the world system. This message will show you how to begin lending instead of always borrowing. You'll be saving and prospering within just a few months after activating this message in your life and finances. **$6.00**

POWERFUL PRINCIPLE OF FILTER AND FOCUS *This message will show you how to filter*

out the good and bad things from your life that are holding you back from your destiny, and to focus on your true calling in life. **$6.00**

TURNING YOUR GREATEST WEAKNESS INTO STRENGTH *This message will*

help you to recognize that your greatest weakness can be turned to your strongest asset by the power of God, as "In your weakness, He is strong"! **$6.00**

(More On Next Page)

Timely Messages On CD
By Dr. Daniel Daves

ARE YOU A JUST CHRISTIAN? *In this message you will find that God is not fair, but He is JUST. There is a world of difference between the two, and once you recognize the JUSTICE of God, you will also begin to judge justly rather than in fairness.* **$6.00**

HE'S BEEN THERE, DONE THAT, AND BOUGHT THE T-SHIRT *No matter what you are going through, He's already been to your tomorrow and He's made provision for you to walk into his blessing and promise.* **$6.00**

GOD IS SHUTTING DOORS AND GOD IS OPENING DOORS *This prophetic word for the body of Christ is one that will activate you successfully into your next move upward.* **$6.00**

Timely Books Available
By Dr. Daniel Daves

"WEALTH TRANSFER"
From The Wicked To The Righteous
You will learn the secrets to success as this booklet shows you how to tap into the wealth of the world system and cause the river of finance to flow freely into your bank account.

English Or Spanish **$4.00**
E-Book – PDF Format - **$3.00**

(More On Next Page)

QUICK ORDER FORM

TITLE	PRICE	QUAN.
Three Keys To Your Next Dimension CD	$ 6.00	_____
How To Cause Earthly Things To Move CD	$ 6.00	_____
How To Lend And Not Borrow CD	$ 6.00	_____
Powerful Principle Of Filter And Focus CD	$ 6.00	_____
Turning Greatest Weakness to Strength CD	$ 6.00	_____
Are You A Just Christian? CD	$ 6.00	_____
He's Been There, Done That CD	$ 6.00	_____
God Is Shutting & Opening Doors CD	$ 6.00	_____
Wealth Transfer Booklet – English	$ 4.00	_____
Wealth Transfer Booklet – English – Book PDF	$ 3.00	_____
Wealth Transfer Booklet – Spanish	$ 4.00	_____
Wealth Transfer Booklet – Spanish E-Book PDF	$ 3.00	_____
The Business Of Ministry – English	$14.99	_____
The Business Of Ministry – English E-Book PDF	$11.99	_____
The Business Of Ministry – Spanish	$14.99	_____
The Business Of Ministry – Spanish E-Book PDF	$11.99	_____

Other titles available at www.basicsforsuccess.com

SPECIAL – Order 4 CD's, **Get One FREE!**

List The Name Of Your Free CD (WHEN PURCHASING 4)

_____

Sponsor A Children's Feeding Program For $5 $_____

Shipping   TOTAL $_____
(Add $5 For First Item, Then $1.50 Per Extra Item)

International Shipping   TOTAL $_____
(Add $15 For First Item, Then $4.00 Per Extra Item)

TOTAL $_____

(Payment Accepted By Check, Cash, Money Order, Mastercard, Visa, Discover, Paypal)

Send Your Email Address If You Are Ordering An E-Book

Send Name, Address, Phone and Payment to:

Mighty Eagle Publishing
8 Calloway Ct.
Mansfield, TX 76063

Or place your order on the web at www.basicsforsuccess.com

Name_____

Address_____

Address_____

City_____

State_____ Zip_____

Phone (_____) _____

Email _____

Credit Card #_____

Expiration Date _____ 3 Digit Code On Back _____

Signature_____
_____ **Yes,** I'd like to be included in your periodic leadership newsletter by email. (Include your email address)
_____ **Yes,** I'm interested in sponsoring a children's feeding program. Please send me more information or contact me.
_____ **Yes,** I'm interested in going on a missions trip with you in the future. Please send me information on your next trip coming up.